Church of the Small Things

Other Books by Melanie Shankle

Sparkly Green Earrings

The Antelope in the Living Room

Nobody's Cuter than You

Church of the Small Things

The Million Little Pieces That Make Up a Life

Melanie Shankle

 ZONDERVAN®

ZONDERVAN

Church of the Small Things
Copyright © 2017 by Melanie Shankle

Requests for information should be addressed to:
Zondervan, *3900 Sparks Dr. SE, Grand Rapids, Michigan 49546*

ISBN 978-0-310-34887-0 (hardcover)

ISBN 978-0-310-35103-0 (international trade paper edition)

ISBN 978-0-310-62932-0 (special edition)

ISBN 978-0-310-35165-8 (audio)

ISBN 978-0-310-34926-6 (ebook)

The author is represented by Alive Literary Agency, 7680 Goddard Street, Suite 200, Colorado Springs, Colorado 80920, www.aliveliteracy.com.

Cover design: Curt Diepenhorst
Cover illustration: Heather Gauthier
Interior design: Kait Lamphere

First printing August 2017 / Printed in the United States of America

To my dad:

This book is for you because you taught me what it means to love family and the importance of being faithful in all the small things that make life worth living. I am grateful for many things and at the top of that list is that you're my dad. I love you more than I can say and have always been so proud to be Charles Marino's daughter.

Contents

Foreword

I met Melanie Shankle on the internet. I laugh as I write that, but it's true. She and I began blogging around the same time many years ago, and fortunately for me, we eventually crossed paths in real life. I felt an immediate connection to Melanie, not just because we were both tackling the brave new world of social media at the same time, but because her unmistakable, irresistibly dry-but-warm humor simply drew me in. One has no choice; just a short conversation and you become an instant Melanie fan.

So Melanie and I are friends. But she also happens to be one of my very favorite writers. Having inhaled her blog and devoured her books for years, I can still plop down, start reading, and find myself laughing within the first five minutes. Melanie has this consistent ability to pull you in with hilarious recollections (usually rich in pop culture references), self-deprecating observations (so, so funny), and family anecdotes that are vividly relatable and real.

But here's the kicker—and the truly magical thing about Melanie: Just when you think the girl is 24/7 funny, she'll throw you a major curveball with a poignant moment. A tender reflection. A spiritual contemplation. A painful memory. And then you have tears in your eyes. The next thing you know, you're crying. (Related note: Have a box of Kleenexes handy as you read certain passages in this book. Consider yourself warned.) But then . . . you guessed it! A classic Melanie one-liner that makes you laugh out loud through the tears. Dolly Parton's character in *Steel Magnolias* had it right: Laughter through tears really *is* the best emotion.

Melanie's previous books have covered motherhood, marriage, and friendship in beautiful detail. But *Church of the Small Things* is, I think, my favorite. With her signature wit and wisdom, Melanie shows us that life is about the small moments, the small memories, the small achievements. We all have them. And when we learn to embrace them, we will see that it really is the small things that make up this beautiful thing called life. As I was reading the manuscript for this book, I sent Melanie a text along the lines of "My gosh, I love this book so much."

It's a good one, friends. I know you'll love it as much as I did.

Ree

Introduction

I've spent my whole life listening to the story in the Bible where Jesus feeds five thousand people with five small loaves of bread and two fish. (Thank goodness that crowd didn't know about being gluten free.) I've seen it depicted on flannel boards in Sunday school, watched it brought to life in movies about Jesus, and heard it taught from various pulpits a million times. Whenever and however the story is told, the focus is always on one of three things: (1) the disciples who didn't have faith in what Jesus could do, (2) the miracle of turning a sack lunch into enough food to feed five thousand people, or (3) the admirable character of the little boy who willingly offered his meager lunch. But you know who never gets a shout-out? The mom who packed that lunch in the first place.

Maybe she was in a hurry; maybe she just threw in those five small loaves and two fish and shooed her boy out the door, glad to get him out from under her feet for the day. If she was like me, she probably hadn't been to the store recently and even gave the fish a quick sniff, worried it might not be any good. Maybe she gave the bread a quick once-over for signs of mold, because how embarrassing would it be to have your kid pull out some moldy bread for lunch? No matter what was involved in packing that lunch on that particular morning, I'm willing to bet she wasn't really concerned or even thinking about how God might choose to use her boy's lunch that day. I bet she didn't wring her hands over whether or not that lunch might matter in the larger scheme of God's plans or wish she could do something on a larger stage in front of an audience of people cheering her on as she tucked that fish and those loaves into a basket, and she definitely didn't do an Instagram story about it. The bottom line is, she didn't do the glamorous thing; she did the faithful thing. She packed a lunch for her boy just like she'd probably done a million times before, and God used her small act of faithfulness to feed five thousand people. He also used her son, whom she'd probably admonished daily to "be kind and share with others," wondering if it was falling on deaf ears. She got tangible proof that day that her boy had actually been paying attention. If you're a mom, then you know that this, in and of itself, can feel like a miracle.

So maybe you can see where I'm headed with this mom and the lunch bag story. Sometimes the biggest things God does start out in the smallest, most ordinary acts of daily faithfulness. The things we do so often and with so little fanfare that we don't even think about them anymore. We can spend so much time wondering and worrying if we're fulfilling God's primary will for our lives. Yet, ultimately, God's will isn't about the things we achieve; it's about the people we become. Life is more about how he uses us to make a difference to the people who cross our paths, even while we are just going about our normal, sometimes boring, lives. He is a God who used twelve men to change an entire world. He is a God who clearly finds value where we tend to look and see nothing special. God's primary will for our lives isn't about a particular job or a circumstance. It's not about the city we live in or whether we're married or single. We are in God's will when we wake up with a willingness to go wherever he leads that day, to seek him in the ordinary, and to love and influence the people around us. Sometimes that can look a whole lot like packing a lunch.

Life is what is happening all around us while we're waiting for the thing we hope will give us some sort of inner peace, contentment, or joy. The problem is that when and if that thing happens, we usually enjoy it for all of three-and-a-half minutes before realizing nothing in us has fundamentally changed. Our hair still doesn't look like Connie Britton's and we're still not as funny as Tina Fey, and so we decide that maybe it's the *next* big moment that will finally make us truly happy. Meanwhile, we're ignoring the fact that we woke up that morning with air in our lungs, had a cup of hot coffee, and laughed on the phone with a friend. I once heard a teenage boy say as he worked at the concession stand at our neighborhood pool, "It's Saturday night and I've got a new pair of shoes—the possibilities are endless." I thought, *Yes! Let's embrace the wonder hidden in the ordinary—whatever the new pair of shoes might be—because these are the moments that are full of possibility and promise.*

Sometimes it happens when we're right in the middle of the daily grind—driving car pool, going to the grocery store, attending class, working in a cubicle, wiping sticky jelly fingerprints off our countertops, tucking in the kids, and packing lunches. One of those normally ungrateful children will hug us extra-tight and whisper, "You're the best mom ever." Or a friend texts to say, "I've been thinking about you." Or we crack up because our insane dog is jumping up repeatedly on the other side of the kitchen window.

When we start to pay attention, we realize life is full of small wonders that can make all the difference in a day, an hour, or a lifetime. And those small moments are no less holy than the big ones. In fact, maybe they are more holy because it is the million little pieces of our lives that really shape the people we become.

In J.R.R. Tolkien's novel *The Hobbit*, the wizard Gandalf says, "Some believe it is only great power that can hold evil in check, but that is not what I've found. It is the small everyday deeds of ordinary folk that keep the darkness at bay." The true joy of life is found in the everyday. It's the moments that don't necessarily take our breath away at the time that often become the ones that matter most. When we look back on our days, we realize such moments are the very threads that make up the tapestry of a life. Taken together, these seemingly ordinary threads of joy, sadness, conflict, and laughter make something extraordinary. With every small thread, God is carefully and thoughtfully weaving a masterpiece.

We live in a culture that celebrates the big accomplishment: the touchdown, the Nobel Peace Prize, the student body president and the homecoming queen. But what if we made it a habit to embrace and celebrate the small? The meal delivered to a sick friend, our kids being kind to the new kid at school, volunteering a few hours a week at a nursing home, or helping someone in need? Savoring a lazy Saturday morning in pajamas, listening to the sound of your children actually getting along, piña coladas and getting caught in the rain?

I've lived long enough to know that often, the most memorable moments in life are the ones that sneak up on you because they weren't planned or orchestrated but are just the simple moments we'll eventually look back on and think of as golden. They are the things of love and parenting and laundry and marriage and what to cook for dinner—just life in all its messy, magical, mundane and marvelous glory. These are the holy moments that are Exhibit A in why I'm a believer in the church of the small things.

These are the stories that, on the surface, may seem like nothing big. Some are silly and some less so, but they are all about the little moments that together leave a legacy and light the way to show us what really matters. A life isn't made from one thing, one big moment, or one huge success. It's created moment by moment, often with pieces that don't look like anything beautiful on their own but are the very fabric of who God meant for us to become as we pack lunches, raise kids, love our neighbors, and simply be who he created us to be—nothing more, nothing less.

Give Me a Casual Corner Suit and Get Out of My Way

Enjoy the little things, for one day you may look back and realize they were the big things.

Robert Brault, *Round Up the Usual Subjects*

It dawned on me the other day that I've lived in San Antonio, Texas, for over twenty years and that I am forty-five years old. For those of you doing the math at home, that means I've lived here almost half my life. Speaking of math, I read the other day that there are three types of people in the world: those who are good at math and those who aren't.

Give yourself a minute to think about that.

The reality is, I have now lived here longer than I ever lived anywhere else, so I guess San Antonio should officially be my hometown. But when people ask where I'm from, I still say Beaumont, which is funny considering I only lived there for six years and have been gone for the last twenty-five. But I guess the city where you went to high school stays a part of your story forever—unlike your grades in high school, for which I am eternally grateful.

I ended up in San Antonio after I graduated from Texas A&M in the spring of 1994. I spent the summer living with my parents in Houston while I went on job interview after job interview, wondering who would be lucky enough to hire a young girl who'd graduated by the very skin of her teeth with a degree in Speech Communications and had a long list of accomplishments on her résumé such as:

September 1992—October 1992: Salesgirl at Limited Express
Assisted customers in choosing outfits for special occasions. In charge of folding and hanging new inventory. (Not mentioned: Basically just stood around and danced to Sir Mix-A-Lot songs.)

July 1993—August 1993: Lifeguard
Responsible for the safety of patrons at the neighborhood swimming pool. Trained in CPR. Also taught swimming lessons to toddlers. (Not mentioned: Basically just sat in the sun and danced to Tony! Toni! Toné! songs.)

While I could sell myself pretty well in an interview setting—thanks to the aforementioned Speech Communications degree—I knew I was dead in the water if they asked to see my college transcript. (Warning to any college students reading this: your college transcript does tend to follow you around, so maybe you should put this book down and go study for that Physics 201 exam.) Anyone who figures out a way to fail Kinesiology 101 isn't exactly a star student, but in my defense, that golf class was dumb and held on way too many days that were better suited to lying by the pool.

I eventually found a job in San Antonio. I credit this to three things: (1) my ability to make myself sound competent, (2) my stellar Casual Corner business suit that screamed "professional career woman" because it was double-breasted, and (3) the fact that the manager who hired me was twenty-seven years old. At the time, I thought she was so mature and wise, but now I know people in their twenties are essentially infants and know almost nothing except what they've learned watching episodes of *Real World* on MTV. I realize *Real World* is no longer a thing, so I guess today's version of it is *Keeping Up with the Kardashians*, and while I'd like to mock this choice, I can't help but feel that my generation started us down the slippery slope of reality television to begin with, and I was one of the first to hop on that train.

Anyway, my first job was working as a contract employee at a local hospital, helping employees figure out how to invest their retirement benefits. Let me stop right here for a minute and ask you to please close this book and look at my picture on the back cover. If I look like someone who gave you financial advice between September 1994 and February 1996, I suggest you immediately have your investment portfolio scrutinized by a certified professional—and I offer my deepest apologies.

Here's what I remember most about that job. My salary was $9,500 a year plus commissions. You would think that the "plus commissions" part would have motivated me to spend more time working as opposed to going back to my apartment for long lunches spent watching the O.J. Simpson murder trial, but you would be wrong.

Side note: When FX aired *American Crime Story: The People v. O.J. Simpson*, I was hooked. It was completely fascinating to watch a movie based on events you vividly remember, which validated for me that those lunch hours spent watching the real trial were totally worth it. Not to overstate it, but it's like I inadvertently made an investment in my future. John Travolta plays Robert Shapiro. Connie Britton plays Faye Resnick. You're welcome.

This also feels like an appropriate time to mention that my best friend, Gulley, was telling her husband, Jon, about a bird she saw in their backyard a few days ago. She correctly identified it as a "red-capped cardinal" and declared herself to be "an orenthalogist." Jon corrected her that she meant "ornithologist," which is the proper term for someone who studies birds, but told her she is indeed also an "orenthalogist" because that describes someone who has spent hours of her life watching a TV series about the murder trial of Orenthal James Simpson. And so, yes, Gulley and I are officially "orenthalogists," and if that is wrong then we don't want to be right.

But back to the story at hand. The problem with $9,500 a year plus the occasional commission check is that it doesn't go far. Especially not for someone who likes the finer things in life, like paying the telephone bill and buying groceries. Not to mention the realization that maybe someone who made a D in Personal Finance 201, was constantly overdrawn on her checking account, and felt like she was playing the lottery anytime she went to the ATM machine (Come on, big money!), didn't need to be in the business of offering financial advice to people who had actual money to invest. So I began looking for a better job in greener pastures like Dallas and Houston. This is probably the first time in history anyone has ever referenced greener pastures in the same sentence as Dallas and Houston because, while they are a lot of things, green isn't one that typically comes to mind. But while I was plotting and planning a job change and a move, something happened. In the words of Elvin Bishop, I fooled around and fell in love.

I met my future husband, Perry, several months before I graduated from Texas A&M. (You can read the whole story in *The Antelope in the Living Room.* Just look for a copy at your local garage sale.) I didn't realize he was also in San Antonio until a mutual friend mentioned it. Perry and I began spending time together mainly because each of us was the only other person our age that we knew in San Antonio, but then it slowly turned into more when neither of us was paying attention. All of a sudden, my master plan to move to another city didn't look quite as compelling. I still knew I wanted to make a job change, though, which is why when my manager pulled me into her office to offer me a promotion, I brilliantly chose to quit my job instead. This is what most career-guidance books and my dad would call a really dumb move. Consider this next sentence the after-school special portion of this book: "Never quit a decent job unless you have another one already lined up, kids."

In what should have come as no surprise, companies were not lining up around the block to hire me. My grade point average ensured that I was shunned like a leper in the twelfth century, and so I ended up with a temporary position in the human resources department at QVC. That's right. QVC, as in the home shopping network. My job was to call people on the phone who'd submitted an application and prescreen them to see if they were qualified enough to bring to the corporate office for an interview. This led to conversations in which I answered questions such as, "Is it a problem that I smoke a lot of weed?" or "I turned in the application for my brother. He gets out of prison on Monday; can he call you back then?" I wish I were joking. The only real upside to working at QVC (or "The Q," as we insiders liked to call it) was the in-house store where employees could shop for deeply discounted items that had been returned by customers. But even that eventually lost its novelty, because a single girl in her twenties doesn't have a great need for dolls from the Marie Osmond Collection or jewelry from Joan Rivers Classics, a fact I'd tend to forget when every time I got carried away thanks to all the low, low prices. (It was kind of like the feeling you get on an airplane when you are desperate and end up looking through the SkyMall catalog because you didn't properly estimate how many *People* and *US* magazines you'd need to get you through the whole flight. That's when your mind tricks you into wondering how you ever survived without an illuminated beverage cooler or a space-saving floor-to-ceiling shoe rack.)

Anyway, my stint at QVC led to job search desperation, and I sent out résumés everywhere and to everyone, but I knew my goal was to stay in San Antonio because LOVE. So I finally resorted to signing up with a corporate headhunter named Sasa Johnson in hopes that she might have better luck finding me a job. I went to her office for my first visit in my most professional Casual Corner suit. She was a petite woman with lots of nervous energy, and I immediately felt like I was in over my head. She scanned my résumé quickly, drumming her fingers on the desk the entire time, and then gave me a steely glance as she looked up and said, "I'm looking at your résumé. I see almost no job experience, no qualifications, and that you graduated from college with barely a 2.0 grade point average. I have to ask, what the hell have you been doing with your life?"

In all fairness, as much as it stung, it was a valid question.

It made me ask myself the same thing as I walked out of her office. It also made me decide to use a different corporate recruiter since it was fairly obvious that Sasa didn't necessarily believe in my potential. Ultimately, I found a job working for a local company that manufactured doors (SNOOZE), but a year at that job gave me much-needed experience and led to a job opportunity in pharmaceutical sales, which is where I spent the next eleven years of my life.

Let's talk for a minute about pharmaceutical sales. I had a love/hate relationship with it. The free car, the nice salary and bonuses, and the incredible health insurance were all huge perks. The days of hauling in lunches from Great China Inn, pretending to be an extrovert in hopes that the nurses would like me, and the constant worry over market share for my products? Not so much. To this day if I find myself sitting in a doctor's office waiting room, I can start to suffer from post-traumatic stress and feel like maybe I was supposed to show up with lunch for thirty from the Olive Garden as I wrack my brain trying to remember the difference between LDL and HDL cholesterol.

But as much as I joke about it, working my way up to a job in pharmaceutical sales was one of the first real goals I set for myself. People tried to tell me it was a hard industry to get into, and I should have majored in Biology (as if), and they only hire people who graduate from college with a 3.5 grade point average or higher. But I didn't let that deter me, because at that time in my life, I saw it as my own little cough and cold promised land. When I got the call from the hiring manager offering me the job,

I realized for the first time what it meant to shoot for something that seems impossible and achieve it. As an added bonus, Perry proposed to me two days later. In the words of Charlie Sheen, I was #winning.

God used that feeling to remind me to trust his voice when, eleven years later, I felt him calling me to walk away from pharmaceutical sales and take a chance on trying to write full time. It seemed like an insane risk at that point in my life, but if you're reading this book then—SPOILER ALERT—it turned out okay.

The point I'm trying to make in this long, fairly uninteresting history of my career trajectory is this: For a long time, I really had no idea what I wanted to do with my life, so I spent years making decisions based on fear rather than taking a leap of faith to figure out what I really wanted to do or who I wanted to be when I grew up. It's what so many of us do, because society has ingrained that kind of thinking into us. We're supposed to go to college, get a degree in business, keep dating the same person, get married, have three kids, buy a house and a minivan, and call it good. It's the American Dream. Except who decided the dream is one size fits all? Especially the part about the minivan. I know they have those automatic doors that slide open, but nevertheless, NO THANK YOU.

Sometimes we get caught up in thinking that the thing God has for us is something huge but hidden, and we either have to work really hard to figure it all out or wait until he drops that thing in our laps like manna from heaven. I absolutely believe God has a plan and a purpose for our lives, otherwise we wouldn't be here. But he has also given all of us unique gifts—time, resources, money, hearts for service, athletic ability, intellect, music, or the dedication to watch all six seasons of *Parenthood* in just a few sittings—which means not one of our lives will look like anyone else's life.

I spent many years wringing my hands over God's will for me and worrying that I was going to miss the whole thing while I was selling doors for a door company or cholesterol drugs for a pharmaceutical corporation. What I realize now is that God used every one of those experiences to build my character, to teach me perseverance and dedication, to help me figure out my strengths and weaknesses, and to shape my perception of the world. He used those jobs to get me to San Antonio, which is where I learned to hear his voice when I was all alone, met my husband, figured out I loved to write, and am now raising my family. I thought it was all about finding a job and being a productive member of society, but ultimately it was God's way of leading me to a home and a purpose.

Nothing is wasted when we view it through the lens of what God has for us in whatever life brings our way. It's all a part of who we are and who he is making us to be. For some, that may be a public role on a big stage, but for the vast majority of us, it's about being faithful in the small stuff: going to the grocery store, volunteering in our kid's classroom, befriending the new girl, coaching a Little League team, showing up for work every day, being kind to our neighbors.

We need to look for God in the ordinary, everyday things, to pursue our dreams and live our lives and be faithful in the small things, because those are the moments that prepare us for the next thing. Pay no mind to the critics who want to point out how and where we might be falling short in the process. I've always loved this quote from Teddy Roosevelt:

It is not the critic who counts . . . the credit belongs to the man who is actually in the arena, whose face is marred by dust and sweat and blood . . .

Or as Taylor Swift taught us, haters gonna hate, hate, hate, but I'm just gonna shake, shake, shake it off.

Or as Sasa Johnson so eloquently asked me twenty years ago, "What the hell are you doing with your life?" Because now I realize what she was really asking—in a not-so-delicate or tactful way—was, "Are you going to waste this one imperfect, yet precious life you've been given?"

Small Things

Things I Wish I'd Known in College

"I was really going to be somebody by the time I was 23."

Lelaina Pierce, *Reality Bites*

Every fall on Facebook, I see pictures of my friends dropping their kids off at college, and it always makes me want to curl up in the fetal position and bawl my eyes out. It also makes me speculate what it will be like someday when Caroline leaves for college, and I think it's probably best summed up in two words: HOT MESS. I have this mental image of her dragging me across the ground as I hold on to her ankles and cry, "Don't leave your mother!" Although the sane part of me knows she has to leave because otherwise, we might become like Big and Little

Edie living with fifty stray cats in *Grey Gardens*, and that's not good for anyone. Maybe especially the cats.

1. It's really never a good idea to drink beer from a funnel.
2. I know Whataburger taquitos are delicious, but perhaps eating them every day at 1:30 a.m. isn't the kindest thing to do to your pants.
3. Those boys who seem like they could have real potential if you could just change a few things about them aren't going to change.
4. On a similar note, not one boy in the history of the world has ever quit calling because he's "scared by how much he cares for you." That's a lie sold by Meg Ryan and romantic comedies in general.
5. Contrary to your belief, you do need to learn how to use a computer, and email is going to take off as a viable form of communication.
6. You will never regret all the late nights you spent hanging out laughing with your roommates.
7. That bodysuit that snaps at the crotch that you insist on wearing with high-waisted jeans and a Brighton belt is a mistake.
8. Maybe you should actually attend class every now and then since that's technically what your parents are paying for every semester.
9. Choosing the right major really doesn't matter as much as just doing enough to graduate.
10. These four years (or five or six) (no judgment here) will teach you more about yourself and life than you ever could have imagined. And give you friends and memories that will still be some of your favorites long after it's over.

How Walmart and a Frito Pie Made All the Difference

> I wish there was a way to know you're in the good old days before you've actually left them.
>
> Andy Bernard, *The Office*

I was born in Houston, Texas, in August of 1971. I'm not sure how familiar you are with Houston, but I will tell you that August isn't one of its finer months—unless you are a person who enjoys breathing air that is so hot and damp it makes you feel like you need to wring out your lungs like a wet sponge.

The story goes that my parents were with the neighbors watching a preseason game between the Houston Oilers and the Dallas Cowboys when my mom realized she was in labor. My dad has always been a fan of football and especially of the Houston Oilers, back when they still existed (Luv ya, Blue!), so I can only imagine the levels of grief he experienced when he realized he was going to have to miss the fourth quarter to get my mom to the hospital.

In what was an early indicator of my night owl ways, I arrived in the world a little after 2 a.m. This was back in the days when the medical profession still treated childbirth with the respect and awe it deserves, considering something the size of a watermelon has just been pushed through something the size of a garden hose, so I assume my mom was knocked out for most of the excitement and I was whisked off to an incubator somewhere for my first few hours in the world. A few days later, it was time for our little family of three to go home from the hospital. My dad brought me a life-size Raggedy Ann doll that I still own to this day, and we made our way home to a one-story brown house complete with wall-to-wall luxurious green shag carpet where I would smile my first smile, take my first steps, and begin to figure out what life is all about.

My parents met in college in the late '60s and married in July of 1969. It seems appropriate that their wedding took place just days after Neil Armstrong set foot on the moon and took "one small step for man, one giant leap for mankind," because my mom and dad truly came from two completely different worlds. In fact, family legend has it that when they first started dating, my mom told her parents my dad's name was Charles Brown. Why? Because the fact that his last name was really Marino would reveal that he was Italian and Catholic, both of which proved to be scandalous to my mom's small-town West Texas family. One could argue here that perhaps Charlie Brown wasn't the most well-thought-out fake moniker, but it just proves that some realities are better than anything you can fabricate in an attempt to write a good story.

Anyway, because the 1960s were an optimistic time, and my parents were both very attractive, I guess they thought all their differences wouldn't matter in the long run. I have no idea about all the ins and outs of their marriage and what went wrong, because those aren't the kind of things you pay attention to when you're a kid. Especially not when you're busy making up scenarios in which your Barbies travel cross-country in a Winnebago, stopping at various destinations to lip-synch Olivia Newton-John songs before returning home to their luxurious townhouse complete with an elevator and an inflatable hot pink couch.

Now that I've been married for almost twenty years myself, I know that every marriage is more complicated than it appears to be on the surface. It can be a delicate dance of romance, hurt feelings, love, driving carpool, cooking dinner, dreams, and a lot of work. It's hard to know why some marriages survive and others don't, other than by some combination of pure stubbornness, grit, and a lot of prayer. A wise, older friend once told me that sometimes the best part of staying married is being glad later that you did, and I think that's about the best marriage advice I've ever heard.

I was eight years old when my parents sat me and my sister down one night and explained that my dad was moving out. It was one of those moments in life that doesn't seem all that significant at the time, but you realize years later that the shockwaves continue to reverberate in countless ways.

Also, when you find you're suddenly one of the few kids with divorced parents in an idyllic suburban neighborhood with tree-lined sidewalks and cul-de-sacs, you quickly realize life is complicated. You learn to be the funny kid to deflect attention away from the fact that you're also the kid who has to have weekly meetings with the guidance counselor because you have some "anger issues." Granted, some of my anger issues were attributed to the fact that I tended to "mouth off" in class with sarcastic comments. As it turns out, that's just my personality.

The next few years were tumultuous. My parents attempted reconciliation at one point, then my mom ended up in an ill-advised second marriage that ended badly and resulted in our moving to Beaumont to be closer to her parents, my Nanny and Big Bob. To this day, Nanny and Big Bob serve as proof to me that sometimes, two complete opposites find each other and figure out how to build a life together.

Big Bob was the youngest child in a family of all girls. His daddy passed away when he was six months old, so Big Bob was raised by his mother and older sisters. I feel certain this was God's way of preparing him for his future, because he married my Nanny and had two daughters, four granddaughters, four great-granddaughters, and one grandson. He spent his life surrounded by women, so he obviously had a high tolerance for pain, lots of talking, and manufactured drama.

He and Nanny were in the same class at Lockney High School. Big Bob was a star football player and sure of himself in that way only a male who's been surrounded by adoring females all his life can be. One night when they were dating, Nanny was waiting for him to pick her up, and he never showed. The next day, she asked him why he stood her up, and he replied, "Oh, I showed up but I saw through the window that you were wearing those pants I don't like, so I left." But for all of his bravado, he couldn't stay away from her. He went off to the University of Texas but missed home and Nanny so much that he came back a semester later.

She had a date with another boy the night he returned but instead, she ran off and eloped with Big Bob. He took her back to his house afterward, and the next morning his mother (who by all accounts was more than a little intimidating) found them in bed together and said, "Well, you've ruined your life."

Big Bob was part of the greatest generation. He served in the Navy during World War II. He left his wife and his little girl to go fight for our freedom. While he was gone, Nanny had the neighbor girls take pinup-style pictures of her in a green bathing suit to send to him. He never talked much about those days, but Nanny said she'll never forget looking outside and seeing him coming up the front walk in his sailor uniform the day he got home. Not surprisingly (especially considering the sailor uniform), my mother was born the next year.

Big Bob worked as an appliance repairman for years. He could fix anything. None of the women in my family ever had to buy a new appliance. He'd just find old ones someone had thrown out, fix them up, and you had yourself a new washing machine.

At any given time, he owned at least three different station wagons. Two were usually Pintos. (I don't think they make them anymore. Mainly because the majority of people don't want a car named after a bean, no matter how tasty.) The other was a huge, full-sized wagon perfect for loading up stray appliances. They all smelled of grease, sweat, and Sir Walter Raleigh pipe tobacco. It's one of the defining smells of my childhood.

My little sister went to a private school, and when Big Bob went to pick her up one day, instead of just stopping at the curb like the other parents, he drove his huge white wagon all the way up the ramp to the front door. Turns out it was raining, and he didn't want her to get wet. She was so embarrassed at his carpool line faux pas that she dove headfirst into the front seat like she had just robbed the place and yelled, "DRIVE, DRIVE, DRIVE!"

In contrast to Big Bob, Nanny had style and always drove

a Cadillac. In high school I would run down the street to her house to borrow her clothes and jewelry because she always had the latest fashions and a collection of twist-a-bead necklaces that would make you weep. I believe the term "bedazzled" was almost exclusively invented to describe her style. Big Bob's fashion sense hovered somewhere in the realm between auto mechanic and Goodwill chic. He was a big fan of the one-piece, zip-front jump-suit, and on especially cold days he paired it with a large fur hat with earflaps. Also, I never saw him without a pipe in his mouth unless he was filling it back up and relighting it.

Most evenings at their house involved Nanny and whichever of her girls happened to be visiting sitting around the kitchen talking while Big Bob sat in his recliner in the living room. He was always quiet, and we thought he was just watching *Walker, Texas Ranger*, but later on he could tell you every word the girls had said. One time, when I was fresh out of college, I was cry-ing to Nanny about how I didn't have any money and felt so overwhelmed. Big Bob was in the other room, but before I left the next day, he handed me $100 without saying a word. He just silently and faithfully took care of the people around him. Looking back, I see that while Nanny often got all the praise because she was right in the middle of everything, Big Bob was always quietly present in the background, navigating the family ship through life like a quiet, steady rudder.

When I was about nine years old, Nanny and Big Bob bought a lake house in Colmesneil, Texas, population 318. Our family wasn't necessarily (and by necessarily, I mean not at all) what you would describe as "outdoorsy" and had never really dreamed of owning any sort of lakefront property until Nanny, who had started selling real estate later in life due to her love of Cadillacs and jewelry, stumbled upon the house when her company listed it for sale. None of us knew the first thing about boats or docks or fishing poles other than what we'd seen in *On Golden Pond*. (And, let's be honest, Katharine Hepburn and Henry Fonda can make anything look dreamy. "The loons, Norman! Look at the loons!")

To our credit, we all jumped in with both feet. Nanny took us up to Granny Graham's Get It and Go, the oldest grocery store I have ever been in, with an equally old Granny Graham sitting behind the counter. (We would always describe her as "even her wrinkles have wrinkles.") Nanny bought us Styrofoam tubs full of night crawlers so we could bait the hooks of our little Zebco poles. We'd sit on the dock for hours with the sun adding to the freckles on our noses while we put worms on our hooks by ourselves, and catch 104 perch in one afternoon. But with every catch we'd yell, "BIG BOB, come get this fish!" And Big Bob would stop whatever he was doing to come take our fish off the line for us and throw them back in the water so we could inevitably catch them again.

We spent weeks there during the summer, floating on inner tubes, going for boat rides, fishing, roasting hot dogs and marshmallows over the campfire, and taking exploratory walks down the long dirt road that led to the highway. One summer my cousin, Todd, built a floating dock that we christened the S.S. Nanny. We'd take it out to the middle of the lake and spend the whole day floating and swimming. Everyone would take turns making runs back to the house to get drinks, pimiento cheese sandwiches, and other assorted snacks. I thought my older cousins were so glamorous and sophisticated as they applied baby oil to their skin while cigarettes dangled from their lips, which were lacquered with a fresh coat of Maybelline, while a jam-box played Waylon and Willie songs in the background.

Some days, Nanny would drive us down the road to Lake Tejas, which was basically the greatest place ever. It was a neighboring lake that had been turned into a real swimming hole. You could rent a tube for a dollar and hang out all day. They had huge slides and the highest high dive I had ever seen. Every summer I had to work up my courage to jump off that high dive, but I always had a fondness for impressing the small town boys, so I'd eventually take a deep breath, make sure my super-cool OP swimsuit was securely in place, and jump. We would spend all day floating and jumping until our fingers were pruney, and then we'd eat Frito pies right out of the Fritos bag before heading home.

Nights at the lake were spent visiting, sitting around on the faux leather couches that stuck to our sunburned legs, and staying up late to watch *The Tonight Show* with Johnny Carson. Most nights, my sister and I could talk Nanny into playing Skip-Bo with us until the wee hours of the morning. The air smelled of the aloe vera and Solarcaine everyone slathered on their sunburned skin, and the face cream Nanny meticulously applied as part of her evening beauty ritual. We were a family full of women, so the house often felt like an offbeat sorority consisting of girls of all different ages. Someone was always crying about something, because at any given time there was someone going through menopause, pregnancy, or puberty. Big Bob always went to bed early, partly because he was an early bird and, I suspect, partly to avoid all the drama.

On days when we'd all had enough of the water and the sun, we drove to Woodville to go to the Walmart. (That's how you know you're in a small town: "the" Walmart, "the" Dairy Queen, "the" Sonic.) We'd load up on essentials like new makeup, a bathing suit, floats, fishing poles, and toys. This was back in the days when Walmart was found only in small towns, so it was a total novelty to city girls. It was also long before I'd experienced the phenomenon now known as "Target Shopping," wherein you walk into a store to buy a bottle of Coppertone and walk out $100 poorer with a cart full of stuff you didn't even know you wanted. We spent hours at the Walmart and were always rewarded with a freshly squeezed lemonade and a corn dog apiece from the stand set up outside the store. Then we'd head home and take a quick swim in the lake before the sun went down. On those nights, we skipped the shower and went to bed with our hair damp from the lake water, warm in our new pajamas from Walmart as the window unit air-conditioning blasted frigid air into the bunk room where we slept on foam mattresses.

Nanny and Big Bob sold the lake house several years before they passed away, but they are both buried in the little cemetery in Colmesneil because the lake house was so much more to our family than just a place to fish or ride a boat. It was a piecemeal house with an odd layout, because rooms were added to make room for more people as my cousins began having families of their own, but it's where real life happened. There were fights in that house; there was always drama; there was the Thanksgiving Big Bob got so tired of all of us that he drank a little more vodka than was reasonable and passed out at the lunch table. It was real, messy, raw life full of love, disappointments, celebrations, anger, laughter, and tears. As a kid who was struggling with what family was supposed to look like, I found it in the waters of that lake and in the walls of that little house.

A few years before Big Bob died, he began to lose his memory. Nanny said she first noticed it when they were at a wedding, and he walked up to her eating a piece of chocolate cake. She asked where he had gotten it, and he said, "Well, it's over there on that table. I just went and cut myself a piece." She said she wanted to crawl under the table when she realized he had been the first one to cut the groom's cake.

During those years, Nanny really needed a break from taking care of him, so my best friend, Gulley, and I drove to Beaumont to stay with Big Bob for the weekend while Nanny drove to Houston to relax with my mom. Around 6 p.m. that first evening, we were sitting with him in the living room when he asked, "Y'all think Nanny's ever going to get out of the bed this morning?" At the end of the weekend when Nanny got home, he told her he'd missed her. She asked, "Where do you think I've been?" and he replied, "Well, I guess you've just been at the Walmart." Which just serves to prove how much time we actually spent at the Walmart in Woodville. Except if she'd really been at the Walmart, she would have brought him some lemonade and a corn dog.

Anytime I spent the night with Nanny and Big Bob, Nanny would kiss me goodnight as she said, "Parting is such sweet sorrow, but we will meet again on the morrow." She and Shakespeare were right; parting is such sweet sorrow. It's weird that you usually don't know life is going to change until it's already happened. I didn't know our last day at the lake would be our last; I didn't know a day would come when we wouldn't go back to the Walmart; and my mind couldn't comprehend that one day Nanny and Big Bob would be gone. Yet here we are.

Their lives and the time I spent with them stand out to me as a shining example that a happy childhood is made up of the small, simple things: a Frito pie, a day spent floating in a tube, a trip to Walmart, and being tucked in at night knowing you are loved.

Things I Wish I'd Known When I Was a Kid

"Are you there, God? It's me, Margaret. I just told my mother I want a bra. Please help me grow, God. You know where."

Judy Blume, *Are You There God? It's Me Margaret*

Early on in my tenure as a mother, I realized one of the joys of having a child is that it allows you to revisit things from your own childhood. The problem with your own childhood is that you have absolutely no bandwidth for realizing life won't always be so simple. It's just one long, endless stream of school days, summer vacations, curling up in a bunk bed next to your best friend while you debate whether you should marry Shaun Cassidy or Donny Osmond, and concluding that eight-track tapes are a technological wonder which will never be improved upon.

Here are a few things I wish I'd known when I was a kid:

1. It's kind of weird that Bert and Ernie live together.
2. Donny Osmond couldn't actually see me through the TV set.
3. When your mom asks, "Who broke this vase?" it's not a real question because she already knows.
4. Enjoy how great you feel wearing a swimsuit, because it's short-lived.
5. Eat more popsicles.

6. There isn't an actual monster living under your bed, and if there were, running and jumping into bed at night isn't really going to help you.

7. If your biggest dream is riding the mechanical bull at Gilley's, then perhaps you should find a bigger dream.

8. On that same note, steakhouses called Tumbleweeds, where they advertise that they'll cut off your tie if you dare to wear one in their restaurant, are just a weird response to the entire *Urban Cowboy* phenomenon and will be a brief fad.

9. Santa Claus will never really just bring a lump of coal.

10. All those choreographed roller skating routines you and your friends create on the driveway will never come to fruition and certainly won't get you a part in *Xanadu II*. And not just because there will never be a *Xanadu II*.

11. Letting your grandmother give you a perm is a bad idea.

12. Cutting off all your hair to sport the "Dorothy Hamill" haircut is also a bad idea. That's a very specific cut for a very specific kind of person, namely an Olympic figure skater or a cartoon character named Buster Brown.

13. Your grandparents won't be around forever. Enjoy the time you have with them and how much they adore you.

14. Baloney sandwiches on white bread with Miracle Whip and crushed Doritos in the middle are gross and will one day be a socially unacceptable thing to eat.

15. There are few joys in life as simple as spending the night with your best friend and staying up late to watch *Grease* for the one-hundred-and-seventy-fourth time.

16. I know you can't wait for your period to start because you've read *Are You There God? It's Me, Margaret* a thousand times,

but once that sucker shows up, it's going to stick around for a long, long time.

17. Don't be in such a hurry to grow up. Childhood is magical and wonderful and the last time you'll ever feel so completely carefree.

18. Someday you will have your own puppy, but you will never have a jukebox in your living room, and it turns out that's probably for the best.

19. Bonne Bell Lip Smackers are still one of the greatest things ever.

20. Your eyes won't really stay like that forever just because you keep crossing them.

3

Yes, Virginia, There Is Such a Thing as a Naugahyde Sofa

That house was a perfect house, whether you like
food or sleep or story-telling or singing, or just sitting
and thinking best, or a pleasant mixture of them all.
Merely to be there was a cure for weariness, fear,
and sadness.

J.R.R. Tolkien, *The Fellowship of the Ring*

We are a soccer family. We spend our weekends at soccer tournaments, we shuttle a car full of junior high girls back and forth to practices three or four times a week, and heaven help us, we record soccer games on the DVR to watch them later. This wasn't something my husband, Perry, and I envisioned for ourselves in our pre-kid days, but let's not even begin to count all the ways parenthood redefines what is important to you. You know what else I never envisioned? That I would know what it's like to catch throw-up in my hands or spend sleepless nights worrying about a twelve-year-old going off to college when it's still six years away.

My career as a soccer mom (because make no mistake about it, this is a second job) began when my daughter, Caroline, was in kindergarten. Her first foray into the world of extracurricular activities involved a short stint in dance classes that caused her to tell us she was "sadder than a pickle that had been eaten," so we decided to make athletics our next stop. The first sport we tried was T-ball, and it quickly became evident that there was way too much sitting on the bench involved for a kid who makes a Tasmanian devil seem lethargic. That's when we found ourselves signing her up for soccer.

What we didn't factor in was that the soccer team was in need of a coach and thus, Perry and I became coaches of a group of five-year-old girls who named their team Rainbow Magic, because everyone knows that there is no more ferocious magic than Rainbow Magic. What they lacked in skill, they more than made up for in candy consumption and overall enthusiasm to move in a huddle down the field as they all vied for a chance to kick the ball. Yet somewhere during that first season, a love of the game was deeply planted in Caroline, and here we are seven years later, consumed by all things soccer.

I tell you this because it explains why we were all gathered around the TV to watch Abby Wambach play her last game on December 16, 2015. She is arguably the greatest women's soccer player of all time, and her accomplishments on the field changed the game forever and fostered a whole generation of little girls who dream of playing soccer at the highest level.

During her last game with the US Women's National Team, Gatorade aired a farewell commercial as a tribute to all Abby

Wambach has meant to women's soccer. It features her cleaning out her locker as she says these words in the background, "Forget me. Forget my number, forget my name, forget I ever existed. Forget the medals won, the records broken, and the sacrifices made. I want to leave a legacy where the ball keeps rolling forward, where the next generation accomplishes things so great that I am no longer remembered."

I love this commercial. In fact, I cried when I saw it for the first time because there is something so powerful about seeing success mixed with true humility and the heart of someone willing to be forgotten so that those coming behind her can achieve even more.

Abby's words have stayed with me, but over time I've decided it's not really possible to forget the great ones whose lives have played out before us. When you have lived life to the fullest, when you've *carpe diem*ed the heck out of who and what God has created you to be, you leave an indelible mark on the people around you and on those who will come long after you're gone.

∽

The summer after my freshman year in college, I lived with my Me-Ma and Pa-Pa. My mom had moved to Oklahoma a few months earlier, my daddy lived in Houston, and I wanted to spend the summer in Beaumont because that's where my friends were. Most importantly, my high school boyfriend, the one I'd been dating for the last two and a half years, was in Beaumont.

It wasn't a good relationship, and in truth, I knew it was on its last legs, but I was eighteen, insecure, and desperate to hang on to anything familiar as everything else in my world changed.

No one really thought I should stay in Beaumont, but Me-Ma and Pa-Pa agreed to let me spend the summer with them on two conditions: I had to go to summer school, and I had to be in by 10:30 every night.

Think about that. I had just finished an entire year with all the freedom college offers, and I was going to spend the summer with a 10:30 curfew, living with my grandparents. Even on the weekends. That is what you call a tight ship. But desperation makes you agree to things you normally wouldn't even consider, and I respected their wishes. And at a time in my life when I certainly wasn't afraid to rebel against authority, I didn't dare break their rules. Back then, I wasn't really sure why I agreed to it, but looking at it now, there is no doubt it's because they were my grandparents, and they adored me and thought the best of me even when I didn't deserve it. I didn't want to disappoint them. They felt like the last bastion of people who truly believed I could do no wrong.

I thought I was staying with them and enduring a 10:30 curfew as a last resort, but I now consider that summer one of the greatest gifts of my life. I'd spent a lot of time with Me-Ma and Pa-Pa ever since we moved to Beaumont when I was twelve, because my daddy drove in from Houston every other weekend and we always spent the weekend at their house, but that summer I got to know them in that way that can only happen when your daily lives are intertwined.

While I'd always felt safe and loved at their house, I saw it through new eyes. Me-Ma and Pa-Pa's house was the unofficial meeting place for all the extended family members, and they came and went all day long almost every day, dropping by without calling first or worrying if it might be a bad time.

Me-Ma never worried about whether or not the house was clean or if she had on makeup. She welcomed everyone with a hug, offered them something to eat, and made them feel so incredibly welcome. She showed me what real hospitality is and that it doesn't involve waiting to have people over until you finally buy a new couch or remodel the bathroom. And, maybe most of all, she showed me that a simple life that revolves around loving your family doesn't equate to a small life.

I had an 8:00 class every morning. I think it was a political science class, but I honestly can't remember because for me, college wasn't so much about the actual classroom experience as it was about the extracurricular activities. Still, I seem to remember some talk of various branches of the government. I'd wake up in the morning and stumble into the kitchen, even though I'd had plenty of sleep the night before, thanks to my 10:30 curfew.

Me-Ma and Pa-Pa would be sitting at the kitchen table, drinking coffee and reading the newspaper. They'd discuss what they needed from Market Basket that day, because heaven knows not a day would pass without at least one trip to the Market Basket since it was the cornerstone of their daily activity.

I'd head off to school and arrive back home around lunchtime. By then Pa-Pa had spent the morning watching *The Price Is Right* and making the first trip of the day to Market Basket. They were gearing up for *General Hospital*, which started at 2:00. The sound of the ambulance in the opening credits of *General Hospital* will always take me back to those afternoons, sitting on one of their Naugahyde sofas, getting caught up in a bad soap opera plot where invariably some girl fell in love with her kidnapper, only to find out he was her long lost brother.

Pa-Pa was a master of various culinary delights. Early on

in my childhood, he introduced me to the artery clogger known as a baloney sandwich on white bread with Miracle Whip and a slice of processed Kraft American cheese. It makes me gag a little thinking about it now. But his real specialty was sausage and potatoes. I'd walk in from class and there he would be, standing over a skillet on the stove, getting it all ready for me. "BIG MEL!" he'd boom. "The cook has your sausage and potatoes going!" I've spent the last twenty years trying to make them like he did and have never even come close. You can replicate a recipe, but there is no substitute for all the love that goes into someone making something for you just because they know it's your favorite and believe you are so perfect that they don't even notice you've gained ten pounds over the course of a few weeks.

That summer ended up being a defining summer for me. I finally broke up with the high school boyfriend, decided to go back to Texas A&M in the fall, and managed to keep my weight at a decent level in spite of all the sausage and potatoes. I watched a lot of *General Hospital* and cried a lot of tears on my Me-Ma's lap.

And I was home by 10:30 every night.

But I think the greatest gift I received that summer was spending every day with two people who thought I'd hung the moon and stars. They built me up and loved me unconditionally when my self-confidence was at an all-time low. They gave me a safe place to land that took me back to childhood for a little while. It was a chance to catch my breath and make some good decisions for the first time in a long time, which gave me the confidence I needed to embrace the future. For that, and for the sausage and potatoes, I will be forever grateful.

As I've thought about Me-Ma and Pa-Pa and how they shaped my life, I realize I can still close my eyes and recall every detail of their home, where I spent so many weekends as a child. It's hard to imagine that a place so familiar, even all these years later, is gone forever.

I remember Sunday afternoon naps on the Naugahyde sofas and, yes, they were as attractive as they sound. I'd fall asleep listening to the sounds of the Houston Oilers playing on TV and wake up with my hair plastered to my face, because let me tell you, that kind of upholstery doesn't breathe well.

I remember the yellow rotary phone that hung on the wall in the kitchen and the plastic fruit that sat in a bowl on a shelf nearby. I used to love to break off the fake grapes and chew on them, which is really kind of gross now that I think about it.

I remember the formal living room that was sectioned off from the rest of the house by a pocket door. That room was never used as much more than a storage facility for a secret stash of premium snack items in the china cabinet. Me-Ma would pull you aside like a Keebler drug dealer and say, "Psst . . . come see what Me-Ma has in here for you," as she pulled out the Nutter Butters or Little Debbie snack cakes.

I remember playing the bubble game in the middle bedroom with my sister. We could entertain ourselves for hours by fanning a huge, king-size sheet up in the air like a parachute and then pouncing down on the big bed to pop the "bubble," while Jesus in Gethsemane looked down on us from an oil painting that hung on the wall. He may have also actually been looking down on us from heaven, but that oil painting made it seem like he was tangibly in the room, which as a kid was a mix of both comforting and creepy.

At night, I slept with Me-Ma in her pink bedroom. (I'm sure at some point she and Pa-Pa shared a room, but those days were long gone by the time I arrived on the scene.) It was the most beautiful room I had ever seen, with its pink walls, pink fluffy bedspread, and gorgeous mahogany four-poster bed. I loved getting out of the bath in the pink bathroom, dusting myself with Me-Ma's pink powder puff, and then climbing into that fancy, pink bed knowing that Me-Ma was going to sleep next to me and would let me stay up late while she read me stories.

I can picture the way the insides of the closets looked; I can see the hallway with its array of family pictures; I can see the garage with Pa-Pa's poker table and picture of dogs playing poker hanging on the wall; and I can see the back patio with its multi-colored tiles, wrought iron table, and statue of Mary looking down on me as I played with my Barbie pool. No doubt the Virgin Mary was probably a little scandalized at all the skin Barbie showed in her yellow bikini.

∾

In her younger days, Me-Ma was a real beauty. I have her wedding portrait hanging in my hallway, and she is so thin, young, and beautiful. By the time I knew Me-Ma, she was obviously older, though I realize now she wasn't as old as I thought at the time. She was plump, had graying hair that she kept dyed black, and wore a lot of polyester pantsuits. She'd raised three boys and lived a lot of life, so she wasn't necessarily thin and fashionable, but man, she was comfortable in her own skin.

I can't think of her without remembering the way she would come hurrying to the door to greet you. She'd have on her turquoise pants, a brightly striped polyester shirt, and some brown SAS orthopedic shoes. She would wipe her hands on her pants because she was always in the middle of cooking something for lunch or dinner. She made the best spaghetti in the whole world, and if I had one more day with her, I'd make her write down the recipe instead of just letting her vaguely talk me through what she put in her sauce. When you left her house, she would stand in the driveway to blow you kisses and give you hand signals like a flight crew to help you navigate as you backed into the street. In spite of the fact that she never learned how to drive, she considered herself an expert at directing traffic.

Me-Ma and Pa-Pa were both first-generation Americans. Their parents immigrated to the United States from Sicily when they were young in search of a better life and landed in Louisiana. They eventually settled in Beaumont, Texas. My dad and step-mom took us to Sicily several years ago, and I can't imagine how depressing it must have been to end up in Beaumont after living somewhere so breathtakingly beautiful, a place that had acres of vineyards as opposed to oil refineries.

Me-Ma married Pa-Pa against her parents' wishes. She was a high school graduate, and he was a sixth grade dropout. She was raised to be a good Catholic girl, and he was a wild bootleg-ger who gambled and ran moonshine back and forth across the Texas-Louisiana border. Her younger sister, Josephina (Fina for short), was scared of Pa-Pa until the day he died. If he answered the phone, she would just hang up and he'd yell to Me-Ma, "That was your dang sister again."

Pa-Pa was a character in every sense of the word. My dad likes to tell us how Pa-Pa would take him to the pool hall while they were supposed to be at Mass. He loved to have a good time.

Despite his limited education, he used his drive and street smarts to provide a nice life for his wife and three sons. And every Friday night, he hosted a poker game in his garage. I remember helping Me-Ma get ready for all of his poker buddies. The garage would be thick with cigar smoke, and I always wondered what went on in there because I was never allowed in. He played poker with the same group of men for as long as I can remember, and the poker games kept going until most of the group passed away and he'd say, "Big Mel, all my poker buddies up and died."

Saturdays and Sundays were always about sports. This was back in the days before picture-in-picture was invented, so my uncles would set up two TVs with rabbit ears balanced precariously on top to get the best picture. A football-watching marathon would ensue, along with phone calls to bookies to make bets. To this day, I take my best Sunday afternoon naps with the sound of a football game in the background.

They had a huge backyard, and Pa-Pa set up two swing sets for the grandkids. We spent more hours than I can recall back there playing baseball using the big oak trees for bases. Pa-Pa would sit and smoke his cigar and watch us play. Every now and then he'd yell, "You kids, don't ruin Pa-Pa's barbecue pit!" or "You kids, don't mess up Pa-Pa's garage!" or "Don't make Pa-Pa go get his strap!" He loved to act put out with us, but I know the truth is he loved every minute of it.

For most of my life, Pa-Pa drove a huge, old baby blue Fleetwood Cadillac. It had an eight-track player that at some point got a Kenny Rogers tape stuck in it, so as you flew down Avenue A at twelve miles per hour, you were always listening to "Ruby, don't take your love to town . . ." And he loved to tell stories. He would sit and tell stories for hours about different things he'd done, and his favorite part was luring us into the story like this: "Do you remember that time we went on that trip with the Modica boy and his dad? How old were you?" My dad would reply, "I think I was ten," and Papa would say, "No, you were twelve." It was like a game show.

Speaking of game shows, Me-Ma and Pa-Pa watched all of them. My love of *The Price Is Right* came from them. And I can't tell you how many Friday nights we watched *Dallas* at their house. True quality programming for the entire family. That's how I learned to throw a drink in someone's face after pouring it from a crystal decanter and that just because you think your husband is dead doesn't mean it won't all turn out to be a dream and you might find him in the shower.

As Pa-Pa got older, he got a little forgetful. A few weeks before I got married, I called to see if they thought they'd make it to the wedding. He answered the phone and we talked, and he assured me he would be there and wouldn't miss it for the world. Then he said, "Let me let you talk to the cook," and as he handed the phone to Me-Ma, I heard her ask, "Who is it?" and he replied "Hell if I know."

Pa-Pa did make it to my wedding, then passed away a month later. One of my biggest regrets is that I didn't make one last trip to Beaumont to see him before he died, but I guess I was busy getting settled into my new life as a married woman. I also believe there was a part of me that was in denial that he was going to die. I'd never lost anyone close to me at that point, and I must have believed he was going to be okay. Especially since he'd spent every Christmas of my life gathering all of us around to announce, "This might be Pa-Pa's last Christmas with y'all." It was a family joke for twenty-five years.

But then he really was gone.

Me-Ma slipped away from us unexpectedly. She had a stroke that just changed something in her. She was okay physically, but something shifted inside and she was never quite the same. She lived four more years and had good days and bad days, but it was like part of her left and never really came back.

Family was everything to them. They were surrounded by the people they loved and who loved them for their entire lives. They knew what was truly important, and their home reflected it. It was very rare that there weren't at least twenty people in their house at any given time. They were always there to laugh at a good joke or old story, to cook a great meal, or read a book to a grandbaby. They loved nothing more than to be right in the middle of all their people, and there was never a day that didn't see Me-Ma wiping her eyes with the corner of her apron as she laughed so hard she started to cry.

What I don't know is why I thought it would never end. I thought we'd always walk up their driveway and Pa-Pa would swivel around in his chair to open the door while Me-Ma hurried toward us from the kitchen, wiping her hands on her clothes, ready to wrap you up in a hug. I know that sounds silly, but when you're young, you take it for granted that things and people will just always be there. You don't realize the richness of a life well-lived and don't question how it all happened.

I've always thought I would love to have one more day with them to ask about their hopes, their dreams, their heartbreaks and disappointments, but I think what I've realized as I've grown older is they probably didn't think much about those things. Life, for the most part, just was what it was . . . good and bad. They lived their lives with a faithfulness and commitment to the small,

important things we tend to overlook in the quest to
thing grand with our lives, somehow missing the fact
small things are ultimately the biggest things.

Me-Ma and Pa-Pa left a legacy of love and steadfastness.
Every day they lived out this command written by the apostle
Paul: "Take your everyday, ordinary life—your sleeping, eating,
going-to-work, and walking-around life—and place it before
God as an offering" (Romans 12:1–2 MSG).

Which brings me back to Abby Wambach's words about leaving a legacy. Me-Ma and Pa-Pa definitely left a legacy that has
kept the ball rolling forward. The generations that have followed
them have done things our great-great-great-grandparents in
Sicily could have never imagined. (And I don't just mean watching Bravo and being able to have take-out food and groceries
delivered right to your door.) But when you've left a legacy that
strong, you can never be forgotten. You shouldn't be forgotten.
Because every moment in what some might consider a small life
was a moment painted with great love.

There is something about grandparents that change and
shape a child's life. Your parents have to work hard and discipline
you to make sure you turn out to be an upstanding member of
society, while your grandparents can relax and let you stay up
late and have that second or eighth ice cream cone. Once you're
good and spoiled rotten, they pack you off you home to let your
parents deal with you. This is called "getting revenge." I can see
so much of my childhood spent with them in my mind and in my
heart, and it makes me a little sad to know that it's all gone, all
part of a bygone era, a piece of time that shaped me and taught
me how to live and love well.

Yet their impact will never be forgotten. Caroline has their bedroom furniture. My sister has their living room furniture. We all have bits and pieces of the things that belonged to them. And more than that, we have the lessons they taught us, the memories they gave us, the stories they told, and the way they loved their family, day in and day out. These are the things they handed down to us when we didn't even know we were paying attention.

Se Habla Van Halen?

The best way to find yourself is to lose yourself in the service of others.

Mahatma Gandhi

I was totally robbed of my First Communion. It's true. I spent the early years of childhood being raised Catholic and going to CCE classes and enjoying all the perks of Catholicism, including but not limited to going to church where they had kneelers you could stand on and pretend to be taller than you actually were. First Communion was something I'd long looked forward to, not because I really understood the holiness of the sacrament, but because it was a significant rite of passage. My Me-Ma used to let my sister and me walk forward with her at her beloved Our Lady of Assumption while she took Communion, until the day my sister blurted out, "ME-MA! THAT MAN DIDN'T GIVE ME ANY OF THAT CANDY!" as we walked the long center aisle back to our seats—and that was the end of that. All of that to say, I had long awaited my chance to walk down that aisle again. But my parents divorced when I was nine, and my mom, who had never converted to Catholicism, began taking my sister and me to a Protestant church. And not just any Protestant church, because all of a sudden we were a hair shy of being arm-waving, speaking-in-tongues Pentecostals. If you want to give a child some serious religious whiplash, this is an excellent way to do it.

So instead of First Communion being a formal affair complete with white patent leather shoes and a frilly white dress from Weiner's and consisting of walking down a long aisle back to a wooden pew while incense filled the air, mine consisted of half a cracker and some grape juice in a thimble-sized, disposable plastic cup while I sat in what was basically a chair from someone's yard because the Protestants lack a little of the pomp and circumstance of the Catholics. And by a little, I mean that our new church met in a double-wide trailer with faux wood paneling and an oscillating fan as opposed to a hallowed cathedral with majestic stained glass windows. Also, instead of First Communion, they called it "The Lord's Supper," which, honestly, sounds like you're about to pull up to a table of meatloaf and mashed potatoes while Jesus calls from the kitchen, "Y'all need anything else?"

But I learned a lot about Jesus within the walls of that double-wide. I learned about the beauty of potluck dinners and that it's always a good bet to avoid a gelatin mold salad, even if the colors are festive. I look back now and think there was maybe a tad bit of misguided teaching going down, but there were also a lot of Sunday school lessons taught on flannel boards that gave me a pretty good foundation of faith to build on.

We stayed at that church until we moved to Beaumont at the end of my sixth-grade year, and after visiting several congregations, we wound up at a church called Cathedral in the Pines. I immediately felt as though I belonged with the youth group there and loved the constant activities. For the first time, church became something I really looked forward to, and I was there every Sunday morning, Sunday night, and Wednesday night. I'm not sure whether my faithful attendance was about an enthusiasm for Jesus as much as it was about all the social opportunities, including cute boys, but there are far worse places for a seventh-grade girl to be than at church, even if her intentions aren't completely pure. God uses mysterious ways to draw us to him, and sometimes that involves a high school boy with gorgeous brown eyes who plays guitar in the youth praise band.

Over the next several years, I did everything with that youth group. Every Sunday night after church, we went to Mazzio's Pizza. To this day the smell of a pizza buffet takes me right back to eating a slice of pepperoni while watching the boys play the Punch-Out!! video game in the arcade. The scenes of my first crushes played out between trips to refill my Dr. Pepper and visits to the bathroom to make sure the enormous lace bow (Shout out to Madonna! As in *Desperately Seeking Susan*, not the mother of Jesus) was still perfectly in place in my hair.

On Sunday mornings, Pastor Dabney used his big, booming voice to preach eloquent sermons from the pulpit as the entire youth group gathered strategically in the last three rows of the sanctuary. We'd pass notes back and forth and, I'm mortified to say, got called out for being disruptive more than a few times. This resulted in threats from our parents that we'd have to sit with them next week instead of our friends, which was, honestly, a horrific fate and enough to ensure our best behavior for a few Sunday mornings thereafter. But eventually, we'd revert back to our note-passing ways—and these weren't just any notes, but elaborate missives in which we actually used countries as code

names on the church bulletins we wrote on in case we accidentally left them behind on the church pew. All anyone would know
if our notes were discovered was that, "Switzerland is still an ally
of the United States, but Russia is looking to cause problems,
which is why Germany needs to be at the movies with us on
Friday night and no one needs to tell the Romanian spies." We
were a United Nations of big church nerds.

During the summer, we went to summer camp, where at
least 85 percent of us would rededicate our lives to Jesus. Again.
Especially after feeling guilty about making out with a blond-
haired boy from another church right before the evening service.
(I'm talking about a friend. Fine. I'm talking about myself. Myself
is the friend.) And then there was always a spring break trip to
a place called Sky Ranch, where we spent three days hurtling
our bodies down water slides, doing our best to tip our canoes
in the lake, and engaging in drama over everything from boys
to friendships. The last night at Sky Ranch always culminated
in a gathering around a big bonfire. This was our opportunity
to stand up and share deep things with the group. There were
always lots of tears and confessions and, ultimately, a whole lot
more rededications to Jesus because our rededication the previous
summer had worn off. Especially when you consider that some
of the stuff we were being taught made us all fear the Rapture
was imminent and there was a good chance we'd be left behind
if Jesus came right after we'd snuck out of our cabins to engage
in shenanigans.

If you didn't grow up in a charismatic, evangelical church,
then I don't think you can truly appreciate how much the Rapture
was a real part of my teenage nightmares and fears. I just knew
it was only a matter of time until I woke up one morning only

to discover that Jesus had returned and taken everyone I knew to heaven with him, and I'd been left behind. You'd think re-dedicating my life to him upwards of fifty-six times between 1983 and 1989 would have given me a little bit of reassurance, but apparently I hadn't quite gotten ahold of concepts like mercy and grace back then. This wasn't helped by reading Christian teen fiction in which a girl could just think about having sex and end up pregnant. Not to mention all the various dramatic skits enacted by the youth group drama team, wherein someone loudly repeated, "TICK TOCK TICK TOCK," in the background as the teens onstage acted out drinking alcohol at a party as a way to remind us that Jesus was coming soon. None of this really helped ease my mind about the whole thing.

Anyway, maybe it was partly fear of not being good enough to be truly saved or fear of missing out on fun (this is most likely), but something caused me to sign up for the youth group mission trip to Reynosa, Mexico, the summer after my freshman year. At that point in my life, I'd never been on any sort of mission trip and probably thought I actually qualified as the less fortunate because I owned only two pair of Guess jeans.

This was back when it still felt fairly safe to travel to Mexican border towns. I mean, sure, there was a good chance you'd see someone selling a goat's head on the side of the road and be bombarded by small children selling Chiclet gum, but that was about the extent of it. So my parents put me in a big blue van and sent me to Mexico. That last sentence sounds like the makings of a fantastic Lifetime movie.

Despite the fact that Texas shares a border with Mexico, it takes approximately nine hours to drive from Beaumont to Reynosa because you are literally traveling all the way across the state of Texas. I'm sure a Texan has never told you this, but we have a big state. We also like to own a lot of things in the shape of our state, but it's not our fault God made Texas in a shape that makes a nice waffle.

Our van caravan was driven by brave, tireless youth workers with a high tolerance for tomfoolery. This was long before the days of cell phones, so our road trip entertainment consisted of occasional stops for fast food and marathon rounds of the alphabet game and Truth or Dare (although there are only so many truths or dares that can happen within the confines of an Econoline van). Several of us also had our Sony Walkmans so we could listen to music. We'd been told that we could only listen to Christian music since this was a church sponsored trip and we were on our way to do the Lord's work, which apparently didn't include listening to Lisa Lisa and Cult Jam. Our musical selections were supposed to consist of artists like Michael W. Smith, Petra, Amy Grant and, for the real Christian rock music pioneers, Rez Band.

However, someone may have slipped in a cassette of Van Halen's *5150* album and caused us all to gather around two earbuds in the back of the van as we listened to "Dreams" over and over again. No offense to any of the Christian artists previously mentioned, but it's hard to compete with an impassioned Sammy Hagar telling you to "dry your eyes, save all the tears you've cried, because that's what dreams are made of." We made our way to Mexico as Sammy Hagar encouraged us to "reach for the golden ring, reach for the sky." That song, along with "Glory of Love" from the *Karate Kid II* soundtrack, were the anthems of my summer of 1986.

When we finally arrived in Reynosa, the temperature was

approximately 158 degrees. I can't remember where we stayed except that it resembled a large dormitory with several rooms of bunk beds and a shared bathroom where we all quickly discovered there was no hot water. Also, there was no air conditioning to speak of, unless you consider two small oscillating fans to be air conditioning, which I personally do not.

Sleep came easy that first night because we were all exhausted from the long trip. We woke up bright and early the next morning, ready to begin our first day of mission work, which was going to involve visiting an orphanage and passing out rice and beans to families in a remote area of town. The girls had been told to wear skirts and dresses, so I put on my cotton Esprit dress with a pair of scrunchy socks and Keds because I wanted to look extra special as I began my first foray into the world of being a missionary.

Nothing could have prepared my fourteen-year-old mind and heart for everything we saw that day. Here was a whole world I didn't know existed apart from the occasional Save the Children commercials narrated by Sally Struthers. I'd never really known what it was to think outside of myself and my little world until this moment. It was both humbling and sobering to spend time with orphans who needed homes, who craved love and attention so much that they congregated around us like we were rock stars even though we were complete strangers.

We spent the next several days painting churches, feeding the hungry, and sharing the love of Jesus with the help of our translators. The thing that amazed me most was how much the people we met wanted Jesus. They were desperate for him in a way that we rarely experience. How desperate can you be if you already have everything you need? The people we encountered that week knew what it really meant when we told them that Jesus was the bread of life because they understood what it meant to be truly hungry, both spiritually and physically.

However, there was one evening when the language barrier caused a little confusion. One of the youth workers spoke to the local church crowd in Spanish, telling them that God was their heavenly father, but instead of using the masculine *el papa*, he said *la papa*. Essentially, he shared a heartfelt message about how our heavenly potato sent his son to save us from our sins. Don't get me wrong, I have had some heavenly potatoes in my time, and not one of them has saved me from my sins. But I still hope they have potatoes in heaven, and frankly, I can't imagine that they don't.

As I've gotten older, I've heard criticisms of short-term mission trips. People question how much good you can do in a few days and whether or not the local people even need their church to be painted or to have a bunch of overly enthusiastic American teenagers teaching their children all the hand motions to *Father Abraham*. (Not to be confused with Abraham the Potato.) And I get it. Sometimes we barge into situations with the best of intentions but don't know how to make the most of our efforts. A short-term mission trip reminds me of that episode of *Friends* when Joey challenges Phoebe to do a good deed that doesn't somehow make her feel better about herself, and she discovers it's impossible to do good for someone else without getting joy from it. Ultimately, she lets a bee sting her, because she forgets that just means the bee will die. Sidenote: There aren't too many situations in life, if any, that I can't relate back to a *Friends* episode. Which just proves that when they sang, "I'll be there for you," they weren't kidding.

Anyway, that trip to Mexico was the first time I understood what it meant to live out these words of Jesus:

> "'For I was hungry and you gave me something to eat, I was thirsty and you gave me something to drink, I was a stranger and you invited me in, I needed clothes and you clothed me, I was sick and you looked after me, I was in prison and you came to visit me.'
>
> Then the righteous will answer him, 'Lord, when did we see you hungry and feed you, or thirsty and give you something to drink? When did we see you a stranger and invite you in, or needing clothes and clothe you? When did we see you sick or in prison and go to visit you?'
>
> The King will reply, 'Truly I tell you, whatever you did for one of the least of these brothers and sisters of mine, you did for me.'" (Matthew 25:35–40)

Sure, I spent a lot of time that week flirting with boys, listening to Van Halen, shopping for cute Mexican embroidered tops in the local market, drinking Big Red, and giggling with my girlfriends late at night, but something also shifted in my heart. Now I could put faces and names with real children who didn't have a home or family. I knew real families who were unbelievably grateful to receive a few bags of rice and beans because it meant the difference in whether or not they'd eat that week. I met local pastors who worked tirelessly to spread the words of Jesus to their congregations, not for money or to build a big building, but purely for the sake of the gospel.

On that trip to Reynosa, my self-absorbed fourteen-year-old heart turned its gaze outward and grew ten sizes. I returned home with a greater appreciation for what I had, including but not limited to air conditioning. That one week laid the groundwork for trips I'd take as an adult to places like the Dominican Republic and Ecuador to serve the people there, to play a game of soccer with kids desperate for love and attention, and to pray with families who have nothing this world says is valuable but do have an unshakable faith that humbles me—especially when they ask how they can pray for us because they have all they need. It made my eyes quicker to see the needs around me and motivated me to figure out how I could help. It gave me a much wider view of the world, one that was very different from what I saw on the streets of my suburban neighborhood.

A few years ago, someone posted this plea on a neighborhood Facebook message board: "Help! Looking for a place to take my kids to feed some homeless people but don't want to have to go all the way downtown!" It made me laugh because, first of all, our neighborhood is five minutes from downtown. Second, I saw myself in that comment because sometimes I want to help, but I just don't want to leave my comfort zone.

Maybe sometimes the point of a mission trip is God changing our hearts and our eyes to see what he sees more than about an orphanage needing us to sing some songs and put on some plays. If our purpose is to become more like Christ, then I think we take the first step on that path when we begin to see things outside of ourselves, no matter how small or insignificant that may sometimes seem. And sometimes we have to leave the comfort of home to get that perspective.

God doesn't call all of us to live our lives on a foreign mission field, but we are all called to help when we can and to love at all times. One week in a small Mexican border town was the beginning of that for me. It created an understanding that there are people in need all around us every day if we ask God to give us his eyes to see them. That week also taught me the words to every song on Van Halen's *5150* album, but, sadly, didn't do much to diminish my fear of the Rapture. Most importantly, that week showed me there can be big implications to small sacrifices of time and resources, whether in a foreign country or in our own communities, and that sometimes the best way to be a light in the world is to shine where you can, when you can, wherever God has placed you.

Things I Wish I'd Known about God When I Was Younger

> You can safely assume you've created God in your own image when it turns out that God hates all the same people you do.
>
> Anne Lamott

1. He's not as angry as some preachers make him out to be.
2. He may or may not look like George Burns, but chances are weighted heavily on the no side of that.
3. He loves us more than we can comprehend.
4. He probably isn't concerned with denominations, the color of carpet in the sanctuary, or whether you have pews or folding chairs.

5. Sometimes he probably looks down here and wishes we'd all quit arguing over stupid stuff that isn't going to matter in light of eternity.

6. He probably thought that bumper sticker that reads "My boss is a Jewish carpenter" was funny the first time he saw it, too.

7. He cares about even the smallest details of our lives.

8. I bet he reads *The Chronicles of Narnia* and thinks "Wow, that's amazing."

9. His mercy and grace are so much deeper than any of us can conceive.

10. His love for me isn't based on my performance, and thank you very much for that, because otherwise I'm sunk.

Why a Trans Am
Might Be Overrated

Listen to your life. See it for the fathomless mystery
that it is. In the boredom and pain of it no less than in
the excitement and gladness: touch, taste, smell your
way to the holy and hidden heart of it because in the
last analysis all moments are key moments, and life
itself is grace.

Frederick Buechner, *Now and Then*

S everal years ago, in a burst of productivity, I decided to
completely rearrange my kitchen cabinets. Now that I think
about it, this may have happened while I was writing my first
book, because I will find any excuse to procrastinate while writing, as evidenced by the fact that I scheduled an appointment to
get a mammogram next week. (Yes, there are days when getting
your boobs manhandled by a complete stranger and squashed in
a hard plastic vise is preferable to trying to put words on a page.
Don't ask me to explain this logic because I cannot.)

At the time, I hadn't cleaned out my kitchen cabinets or

changed the way things were arranged in almost ten years, and eventually I realized there had to be a better way to use all that space. There was one huge corner cabinet that held nothing but our wedding china and stemware, which had been used approximately three times in eighteen years of marriage, so I decided I should move all that stuff my mother-in-law said I'd be happy to have someday to the cabinets above my oven, which is totally out of normal reach and a much better location for crystal goblets that might still have price tags on the bottom of them.

So up went all the Lenox china, and I never really thought about it except on the occasions I'd open that cabinet to pull out a terracotta chip and dip tray that was a wedding present I actually use because CHIPS AND DIP. But then last week I went to pull out the chip and dip tray because it was the Super Bowl (I mean the Super Bowl as in the one where they play professional football, although the chip and dip tray is very much its own super bowl in a matter of speaking), and I noticed it was filled with broken pieces of crystal stemware. On further inspection, I realized the cabinet had completely shifted, causing the back shelf to crash down and break several goblets. As I surveyed the mess, I was much sadder about having to spend time cleaning up the broken pieces of glass than I was about the actual glasses, because you know what? My twenty-five-year-old self picked out those pieces of Waterford and fine china for some idea of what I thought real adult married life would look like. That idea was largely based on the fact that I spent a lot of my formative years watching *Dallas, Dynasty,* and *Falcon Crest,* all shows in which there was never any shortage of people pouring scotch from crystal decanters into fancy glassware.

It made me think about all the ways pop culture in the 1970s and early 1980s influenced my thinking about exactly what my adult life might look like. Most of it has turned out to be completely inaccurate. Let's take a closer look.

1. *Grease* (the musical, not the laundry stain)

I have seen this movie upwards of 473 times. I owned the sound-track on both eight-track cassette and a double record album with bonus photos inside. I dressed as Bad Sandy for at least three Halloweens and can't guarantee I won't do it again in the future, except that my time of looking remotely appealing in black spandex is quickly diminishing.

There was a time when I came up with a master plan to be the good girl and wear skirts all year long and then show up on the last day of school wearing some Jordache jeans and my Nike tennis shoes and shock the entire third grade class at Bammel Elementary School. Which, granted, is not exactly as cool as showing up in black leather pants and red Candies, but I was a realist. I knew my mom would never buy me black leather pants because—hello—inappropriate. But that didn't keep me from cutting up some black leotards and tights and wearing them with my mom's Candies to reenact that last scene over and over again. And really, is there anything more appealing than a seven-year-old pretending to put out a cigarette with the toe of her high-heeled shoe while saying, "Tell me about it, Stud"?

(Note to self: Do not allow Caroline to watch *Grease* until college.)

Grease was the reason I believed I'd meet my true love in high school, he'd wear a leather jacket and be part of a cool gang, and, after a festive carnival to celebrate the end of our senior year—during which I totally changed to be what he wanted me to be—we would drive off together and inevitably live happily ever after. What could possibly go wrong?

2. *Coal Miner's Daughter*

Do not try to convince me that this isn't one of the greatest movies ever made. I will sit and watch the entire thing anytime it's on TV. What other movie has even come close to offering such classic lines as, "Hey, Doolittle Lynn, who's that sow you got wallowin' in your Jeep?"

For many years I wanted to travel the country in a car with my husband as we looked for radio stations and asked them to play my album. Ultimately I'd end up singing at the Grand Ole Opry and wear long, ruffled dresses. I'm sure the only thing that kept all of this from actually happening is the little detail concerning my lack of a singing voice.

3. *Urban Cowboy*

Nothing is more romantic than getting in fights at honky-tonks and riding mechanical bulls, right? For years after I saw this movie, I dreamed about my wedding day and just knew I'd have the band play "Could I Have This Dance?" by Anne Murray.

I'd wear white cowboy boots with my wedding dress before we moved into our brand-new double-wide trailer, and we'd spend our days training for mechanical bull riding contests. To my credit, I had no desire to repeat the part about hooking up with an ex-convict who stole money from Gilley's and wore shirts made out of fishing net—I had standards, after all.

4. *Smokey and the Bandit*

I don't know what I loved more, Burt Reynolds or that black Trans Am he drove. I do remember that my sister had a crush on Jerry Reed, and we'd argue about who was cuter, Bandit or Snowman. Also, it made me want a CB radio in our car more than anything in the world. Oh, the elusive glamour of being known on the interstate by a super classy handle like "Hot Pants."

As I look at the common thread running through most of these movies, it appears I essentially wanted to grow up to be a redneck who traveled the country in some form in "hot pursuit" of something. But you have to realize no good can really come of running out on your wedding day and hopping into a black Trans Am driven by a lawless cowboy running beer across state lines in a race to win a bet with a father/son duo known as Big and Little Enos.

5. *The Electric Horseman*

This movie was pivotal, if for no other reason than how good Jane Fonda looked wearing her jeans tucked into her boots. It inspired my fashion sense at an age when my wardrobe consisted largely of Luv-It jeans with embroidered roller skates on the back pocket. It also made me think that maybe one day, I might run off with a rodeo cowboy trying to save a racehorse from a life of drugs and being paraded on a stage lit up with Christmas lights. We'd end up in a canyon in Montana watching wild mustangs run while Willie Nelson sang in the background, "My Heroes Have Always Been Cowboys."

Perhaps I'm saddest that this particular version of adulthood never transpired because that sounds fairly dreamy even as I sit here watching my daughter's soccer practice and reminiscing about it. So I guess the lesson here is that rodeo cowboys who wear light-up suits trump mechanical bull riders and Trans Am drivers every time.

No. Sorry. I don't think that's really the lesson here.

Well. Maybe a little, but not the one I'm looking for at this particular juncture.

The point is, when I was younger, I pieced together all these fantasy versions of what I imagined real life would be like, and decided it looked a lot like being a secretary who rides mechanical bulls, disco dancing in flowy dresses with a man wearing a white suit, and singing at the Grand Ole Opry before riding off into the sunset in a black Trans Am to set a horse free in a canyon in Montana. And listen, if any of those describe your life, then let me be the first to say WELL DONE. I applaud you and the fantastic choices you have made. Clearly.

The truth is, I sit here at forty-five years old, and my life, for better or for worse, bears no resemblance to any of the aforementioned scenarios. I can still hope that maybe singing onstage at the Grand Ole Opry is in my future, but chances are it's not going to happen and not just because I have no discernible singing talent. My days consist largely of waking up to an alarm at way too early o'clock, starting a load of laundry I meant to start the night before, deciding what kind of meat to thaw for dinner, cooking a bowl of oatmeal, packing a lunch, and driving a teenager who may or may not be having the worst morning ever to school before I return home to clean up the kitchen, make a grocery list, and convince myself that maybe I should actually go work out since I'm wearing workout clothes for the seventeenth day in a row. Some days I feel like I'm doing a pretty good job at being a wife, mother, daughter, and friend; and some days I feel like I want to run away from home because I am an idiot who is just screwing everything up.

Perry and I were watching beach volleyball during the Summer Olympics awhile back, and the announcers were talking about Kerri Walsh Jennings and her incredible career as a beach volleyball champion. They aired a voice-over of her saying that she strives to be the best at everything she does: the best wife, the best mother, the best athlete. Perry turned to me and said, "I bet it wouldn't be very fun to be married to her." (It's a smart man who knows to say that to his wife while watching a gorgeous blonde with zero percent body fat in two strips of fabric play volleyball.) But I was curious about his thought process and asked why he'd said that. He replied, "It sounds like a lot of trying. I bet it gets exhausting." I turned to him, grabbed his hand, and whispered softly, "Here is my promise to you. I will NEVER try to be the best wife."

The truth is that real life is messier than the movies, and sometimes the harder we try to make everything look a certain way, the more frustrated we find ourselves. There isn't always a happy ending, the boy doesn't always get the girl, the marriage doesn't always work out, the kids don't always learn their lesson, and Prince Charming may never come riding up in a light-up suit on a rodeo horse. So I guess the question becomes, *Is my real life better than what I imagined it might be back in 1981 based on what I saw on a movie screen?*

The honest answer is *yes* on most days. I love my family. I love my friends. I love this life I've been given, and I don't take it for granted. But occasionally, when Caroline is having a level-ten reaction over Algebra homework and I have to think of a new way to cook chicken for dinner and the dog has just thrown up on the rug, I look out the kitchen window longingly, wondering what it would be like if Burt Reynolds showed up in a black Trans Am.

6

The Dirty Truth
of a White Couch

It does not do to dwell on dreams and forget to live.

Albus Dumbledore, *Harry Potter
and the Sorcerer's Stone*

It starts when we are little girls. We see Cinderella find her Prince Charming, Sleeping Beauty awakened by true love's kiss, and best of all, Snow White living with seven dwarves who whistle while they work, and we think to ourselves, "How can I have that?" Eventually we graduate to more sophisticated and complicated love stories that play out on our movie and TV screens, and we wonder why not one man has ever barged into girls' night at our house and declared, "You complete me."

The truth is, real life doesn't usually resemble what we see on any kind of screen, especially the big screen. There are dishes to be washed, beds to be made, and laundry to be done, and no one wants to see a movie about that. Also, can we talk for just a minute about the laundry? It never ends. I didn't understand for a long time that the real reason I only had one child was because God knew I couldn't handle the laundry for any more than that, but I know it now without a doubt. The laundry will cause your soul to shrivel up and die because it's a battle you can't win. Are you sitting on your couch right now feeling smug because you believe you've actually washed and put away all your family's clothes? Then let me ask you a question. Are you wearing clothes right now? Did you send your kids off to school wearing clothes? I hate to be the bearer of bad news, but all those things are now dirty laundry. It never ends.

Whether you are married or single, have kids or are childless, work from home or in an office, volunteer for the PTO or just watch a lot of Netflix on your couch, life has its ups and downs. It's messy and hard and beautiful and wonderful, sometimes all within one hour. If I could sit down across from you (and I so wish we could make this happen), I would share that perhaps the thing I've learned the most over the last several years is that we all have a tendency to compare our lives to others' and think everyone is living a better story than we are. With social media, it's never been easier to get a glimpse into strangers' lives and decide their marriage is better, their house is cleaner, their kids are better behaved, while we are just a step away from living in a van down by the river and we don't even care because our children are so ill-behaved that it would seem like a vacation.

I've read so many articles about what porn does to a man and why it's so damaging, but as women we deal in some form of what might be called "emotional pornography" all the time—often with-out even realizing it. We fantasize about how life would be so perfect *if only* we had that new couch from Pottery Barn, *if only* our kids wore smocked dresses instead of that same old Gap T-shirt with the stain on the front, or *if only* we could finally lose that last ten (okay, fifteen) pounds of baby weight and fit back into our skinny jeans.

About three years ago, I made a mistake of epic proportions and let an interior designer friend talk me into buying a white couch. I really can't put the sole blame for this purchase on her, though, because the truth is I'd been pinning white couches on Pinterest for months along with doing Google searches like "How hard is it to clean a white couch?" "Am I crazy for wanting a white couch?" and "White couch: friend or foe?"

Every blog post I read by someone who'd made the decision to buy a white slipcovered couch raved about how it was just so easy to maintain. Sure it gets dirty, but you just take those slipcovers off, throw them in the washing machine with some bleach, toss them in the dryer, and your couch is as good as new! As good as new! In fact, it's even better because you have the smug satisfaction of knowing your couch is cleaner than your neighbor's couch because who knows what horrors lie within that dark taupe fabric that the eye can't see.

So I drank the Kool-Aid and bought a white couch. Ironically, I could never drink actual Kool-Aid on the white couch, because there are some stains that cut too deep—specifically stains from powdered drink mixes that can also be used to dye hair.

The day the white couch was delivered was perhaps second only to the day my daughter was born on the scale of best days ever. My living room looked like it was ripped straight from the pins of Pinterest. (If it weren't for Pinterest, none of us would know that there is actually a decorating style called "Vintage Industrial Train Station," so basically Pinterest was created for the purpose of making women everywhere feel like we aren't living up to our potential.) And for that one glorious day—let's be honest, it was more like two hours—I defied every teacher I'd had throughout school who wrote, "Does not work to full potential"

on my report cards because I was—as Whitney Houston sang—
EVERY WOMAN. It was all in me.

I strategically placed my multi-colored throw pillows on that
white couch and then took a slew of pictures to post on my blog,
Instagram, and Pinterest, because if an awesome white couch
falls in the forest and no one is there to see it, does it really exist?

Then life happened. Perry came home from a long day of
landscaping work and innocently sat on the couch to try it out,
leaving behind a bottom imprint made of dust and grime. "OH
NO! THE COUCH!" I cried as I wiped my hand across the cushion furiously, trying to erase the dirty mark. Perry glanced at
me with a look of pity as he remarked, "Well, this couch is going
to work out beautifully. Totally worth the money because who
needs a couch you can actually sit on? That's for regular people."

I realized I'd made a tactical wife error so I immediately
switched into a more laid-back mode. "Well, the beauty of this is
it's all slipcovered! It's a wash-and-wear couch! It doesn't matter
if it gets dirty because I'll just wash it with bleach and it will
be brand-new again! This is the best money we've ever spent!
I promise! It's all fine! Everything is fine!" A week later, I had
some girlfriends over for a wine night, and one of them accidentally spilled almost an entire glass of Cabernet on the center
cushion. I played the role of gracious hostess as I explained, "It's
no big deal because BLEACH!"

The next morning, I stripped all the slipcovers off, washed
and bleached them for the first time, threw them in the dryer
and then began putting them all back on the cushions. That's
when I discovered all those white couch evangelists are either
gluttons for punishment or in much better physical shape than I
am because people have finished triathlons with less sweat and

exertion than it took me to get those slipcovers back on the cushions. There was profanity involved. I tore my clothes and covered myself in sackcloth and ashes when it was all over. What fresh hell hath Pinterest and my pride wrought?

I couldn't admit to Perry that I'd made a costly, tactical error. Even as he occasionally declared, "Babe, we aren't white couch people," I insisted we were. We are clean. We shower. And look how good that couch looks for all of thirty-eight seconds once every three months when I muster the inner fortitude to wash, dry, and repeat.

Then we brought home two new puppies, Piper and Mabel, who developed a penchant for flying through our back door and making a running leap onto the white couch, muddy paw prints be hanged. This was the final straw that proved to be the tipping point of my delicate grasp on sanity, which resulted in a tearful confession to Perry: "I can't do this. I cannot live like this. BABE, WE ARE NOT WHITE COUCH PEOPLE! ERRBODY BE SO TIRED OF THIS WHITE COUCH!"

He hugged me, and I'm sure there were all manner of "I told you so" comments raging inside his head, but he is a smart man and just said, "Why don't we look into getting a new couch?" And with that, I ordered a new brown leather couch so fast it would make your head spin. Brown. I wanted all brown. I am a brown-couch-that-can-be-wiped-clean-with-some-leather-cleaner kind of person. It's not nearly as Pinterest-worthy but it helped me quit walking around like a woman in need of a lot of medication, although I continued to be a little disappointed that I wasn't up to the white couch challenge. Maybe those teachers were right after all, and I'm not living up to my potential.

But you know what I was doing with all my visions of what life should be, could be, and ought to be based on Pinterest and bad movies from the '70s and '80s? You know what we all do when we sit around thinking about our Fantasy Someday?

We miss the holiness of this moment we're living right now.

There will never be another one like it. And even if that makes you think "THANK GOD, BECAUSE MY LIFE CURRENTLY STINKS," there are still lessons to be learned, character to be built, and stories that will be told about where you are right now. God takes all of it—the mundane and the ugly, the clean couch and the wine spills, the ordinary and the occasional extraordinary—and when we allow him to add his grace, his mercy, and his outrageous love, he adds a brushstroke there and some color here and so paints it all into one glorious work of art, one that only he can achieve through us where we are right in that moment—in our homes, in our neighborhoods, in our classrooms, in our communities and world. No one else can live our story. So maybe it's time to embrace all that is uniquely ours and realize that is exactly what makes it special.

——————— *Small Things* ———————

Things I Wish I'd Known in High School

You see us as you want to see us—in the simplest terms, in the most convenient definitions. But what we found out is that each one of us is a brain . . . and an athlete . . . and a basket case . . . a princess . . . and a criminal. Does that answer your question?

The Breakfast Club

A few years back, I received an email about plans for my twentieth high school reunion. My first thought was, bless their hearts, it hasn't been twenty years since we graduated from high school because that would mean we're old and all drive minivans and wear sensible loafers. Then I did the math and realized that yes, as a graduate of the class of 1989, it had been twenty years since I teased the crap out of my bangs in hopes that they would be higher than my mortarboard cap when I walked across the stage to receive my diploma and hugged all my classmates while a cassette tape of Whitney Houston belted out "One Moment in Time" over a mediocre sound system.

Then I looked in the mirror and found two new gray hairs.

And then I cried.

One of the things the reunion planners asked was that we send in any old pictures we had from our high school days. As I looked through my high school photo album full of memories, I reflected on all the things I'd learned over the last twenty years. Deep life lessons. The wisdom that only comes with age and the realization that Guess overalls can't bring lasting happiness, even though they were totally awesome when I wore them with my Esprit booties.

Here are twenty other lessons I've learned over the last two decades.

1. Tweezers are your friend. For heaven's sake, if your eyebrows cover half your eyelids and often impede your vision, don't be afraid to get rid of a few of them.
2. It may seem cool to get a car with only two seats, but it will prove to be impractical even though it has a sweet Alpine stereo system with a radio that requires you to turn the knob to change stations.
3. Nautical-themed attire is best reserved for toddlers and sailors.

4. Four perms a year is four perms too many.

5. Later in life you may experience some guilt related to your direct role in destroying the ozone layer due to excessive use of Rave aerosol hairspray.

6. Tucking your jeans into your socks just makes you look like an ice cream cone. An ice cream cone with a big, crispy perm on top.

7. Blue mascara. No.

8. Lying out in the sun using only the SPF contained in baby oil is a bad idea. (Why did it never occur to me that I was literally frying myself?)

9. It's possible to wear too much Lauren by Ralph Lauren perfume, especially if you carry it around in your purse to touch up your scent between classes.

10. Just because you can get shoes dyed to match your peach lamé prom dress doesn't mean you should. And really, peach lamé is a regretful choice.

11. Peplums don't work for everyone.

12. Same goes for shoulder pads.

13. Contrary to your belief, Erasure will not prove to be the best band ever. Ditto for Duran Duran and Whitesnake. However, Run DMC and The Beastie Boys totally stand the test of time.

14. While satisfying and delicious, a lunch comprised of Cool Ranch Doritos and Reese's Peanut Butter Cups probably isn't the best choice.

15. As it turns out, breaking up with a boyfriend doesn't mean it's the end of the world, although it does push the limits of how many times you can fast-forward a mix tape to Sinead O'Connor singing "Nothing Compares 2 U" or listen to the entire *Chicago 17* album.

16. There is such a thing as hair that's too big. A sure sign is when it extends past the perimeter of your graduation cap or requires you to use a whole bottle of Aussie Sprunch Spray and a set of fifty-two hot rollers to achieve the desired width-to-height ratio. Sometimes less is more.

17. Same goes for bows—on dresses and in your hair. Also, a puffed sleeve should be used in moderation.

18. The banana clip was an unfortunate hair accessory made more unfortunate by the fact that you owned one in every color.

19. You were never more right than when you informed your geometry teacher that geometry was a waste of time because you'd never use it in real life. EVER.

20. Twenty years go by in the blink of an eye, and while each one has its share of challenges, life just gets better.

Out of curiosity and interest in the male perspective, I asked Perry what he's learned since high school and he said, "You reap what you sow." I was thinking more along the lines of, does he regret having a mullet during his junior year of high school? So I guess the other life lesson is, it's a good idea to marry someone who tends to be a little more philosophical and introspective about life, although I think it's safe to say, in retrospect, the mullet was a bad call.

Forty Is Not the
New Thirty

Life is amazing. And then it's awful. And then it's amazing again. And in between the amazing and the awful, it's ordinary and mundane and routine. Breathe in the amazing, hold on through the awful, and relax and exhale during the ordinary. That's just living, heartbreaking, soul-healing, amazing, awful, ordinary life. And it's breathtakingly beautiful.

L.R. Knost

or

It's hell to get old.

Emiel Marino, also known as my Pa-Pa

I just spent a few minutes reading an online article about twenty-five celebrities who haven't aged well. Of course, using the term "article" is a generous assessment of what was essentially a slideshow of photos that showed various celebrities as their youngest, best selves contrasted with a more recent photo taken when

84

they were most likely unaware of the camera's presence, weren't wearing a stitch of makeup, and had decided it was a good day to breathe through their mouths. But this is the kind of "article" that sucks me right in because I am all about some serious, hard-hitting journalism regarding plastic surgery gone wrong.

Make no mistake, we have become a people who believe in some cosmetic overhauls. Aging naturally is for suckers. I think I first realized it was an epidemic when I watched *Real Housewives of Orange County*. They all had to drink their cocktails through straws because not a one of them could trust that their lips had enough feeling left in them to support the whole notion of actually drinking from a glass. At first glance, I found myself thinking, "Well, that is a lovely forty-year-old woman without any wrinkles," but then realized it was actually a twenty-nine-year-old with Botox who just looked like a well-preserved older woman because her face didn't make expressions anymore, and between the bleached blonde hair and the enhancements, it's hard to tell a thirty-year-old from a sixty-year-old.

And I'm not even saying I'm against the Botox or the Restylane or whatever else is out there that serves as a proverbial fountain of youth. In fact, there have been times I've considered it myself. Like the time Caroline examined my forehead closely one morning and rubbed it with her little fingers before exclaiming, "Mom! I can see your brains on your forehead!" Really? Because I can see me dropping you off at a fire station to see if you can be adopted.

My bathroom cabinet is now full of products that all make varying promises to give me a youthful glow and reduce fine lines, deep lines, and hyperpigmentation. They guarantee that after four weeks, I will see a reduction in sagginess, wrinkles, and depression when I look in the mirror. They will lift, tuck, refresh, and restore my face to some version of what it used to be. I have never used more products on my face than I do at this stage of life, and it all seems a little bit like trying to build a sand castle right where the tide is rushing in. You can pile and shovel and scoop on everything you want, but it's just a matter of time before nature wins out and that whole thing collapses.

Also, you don't even want to know the font size I'm typing this in just so I can read my words on the screen. The other night I had to use my new readers *and* the flashlight on my iPhone to see the words in the book I was reading, and all I could think about was how I used to make fun of my grandmother for asking waiters at restaurants if they could turn up the lights or bring over a flashlight so she could read the menu. Now I am that person.

People want to tell you that forty is the new thirty. You are young, you are vibrant, you are better than ever! And I do believe that might be true mentally, but I can assure you it doesn't apply to your physical state, particularly and maybe most assuredly to your metabolism. My face is decidedly not better than ever with the ramifications of my ill-spent youth in the sun dotted all over my complexion. And my ankles pop every morning when I hit the floor. I really can't even talk about my knees. They don't look or feel the way they did five years ago. I'd like to say I look in the mirror and see my grandmother's knees, but the truth is I think I see Snuffleupagus's knees. Except I shave mine.

Not to mention all the pressure to celebrate the big 4–0 milestone with a huge party. As soon as I turned thirty-nine, everyone began to ask what I was doing for my fortieth birthday. I didn't know. Maybe staying home in my pajamas and reading *People* magazine before I turn on Netflix and have two glasses of wine because it's my special day? Some of us introverted types like to party like rock stars. Rock stars who don't actually party as much as just hole up in fancy hotel rooms and watch TV. Can't you just leave us alone and let us commemorate the day without any social pressure? We're happy with that. I promise. We really are. Because the mere thought of turning up at a surprise party for myself filled with all manner of my friends from different stages of life is enough to cause me to breathe into a paper bag. That's the kind of thing that needs some advance warning. I realize there are those who love nothing more than a huge celebration, and I dearly love some of those very people, and I'm happy to celebrate with them as long as *they* are the center of attention. I just don't know why there's all this pressure to celebrate the end of the thirties with a huge middle-age palooza when some of us are just lame enough to spend it reading a good book.

I recently spoke to a group of college students at Texas A&M University (my beloved alma mater). I always enjoy college-aged kids because they are what I like to call "amateur grown-ups". They have some responsibility in life; they have to get themselves to class and buy their own groceries and pay their bills, albeit for most of them it's with money their parents have put in their bank accounts. But then they have this whole other side of life where they can stay out until 2 a.m. on a Wednesday night and eat Taco Bell every day and go watch a baseball game with all their friends on a Tuesday afternoon. For me, college was one of the best times of my life. It's a good thing none of us know how great we really have it during those years or we would never graduate, and then who would pay for all the fun? Plus, who wants a bunch of forty-year-olds in their sorority?

I kept telling them all how cute they were, which is such an old-person thing to say. I was one step away from pinching their cheeks when I said it. But I couldn't help it. They were so cute and so fun and so full of life.

The other speakers at the event were a Stage 4 colon cancer patient who finished the Ironman World Championship after being diagnosed and a man who owns a hugely successful public relations firm in Washington, D.C., and whose life changed dramatically after he almost drowned in the Persian Gulf.

And then there was me. One time I had to pay full price at Gap and my dry-cleaning wasn't ready when I went to pick it up. There was also that time I forgot to charge my Clarisonic skin brush and had to wash my face with my hands. We have all had our personal struggles. I think it was mainly my job to let the students know that you can score a thirteen on a college exam and it isn't the end of the world. Ask me how I know.

As I looked around that room and spoke to many of the students afterward, I just wanted to wrap them all in a big hug and tell them the next five to ten years might be a little rough, but they should hang in there. And wear sunscreen. The truth is, it can be easy to idealize what those years were like because there was much fun to be had, but I wouldn't go back to my twenties for anything unless you could send me back with the knowledge I have now. Kind of like Michael J. Fox in *Back to the Future* but without the puffy vest. Or maybe with the puffy vest, because I do enjoy a vest on occasion.

For most of us, the twenties are all about figuring out what life is about separate from our parents. What kind of career do we want? Where do we want to live? Who do we want to marry? Sure, we have great skin and toned legs, but we're too filled with angst to enjoy it most of the time because we're learning that adulting can be serious business with good and bad consequences.

By the time most of us deal with the decisions of our twenties, they are over.

The thirties for me were all about settling into married life, becoming a mother, learning how to get the smell of a rotten sippy cup filled with old milk out of my car, and trading in corporate life to be a homeroom mom. They were about finding my way and getting used to being called "ma'am" and realizing it took more than giving up chocolate ice cream for two days to lose five pounds.

Those were the years that sometimes seemed endless, with a toddler who wouldn't nap, finances that always seemed to be an issue, and marital struggles that became more real as the shiny newness of our wedding rings faded and we had to figure out bigger things than what we were going to have for dinner that night.

And now here I am, smack-dab in my mid-forties. I vividly remember thinking people in their forties were old and probably spent a lot of time watching episodes of *Murder, She Wrote* after eating dinner at Golden Corral. I thought a lot about turning forty before I got here, and then an older friend of mine encouraged me that the forties are a kind of crossing over for a woman, a new beginning of sorts. I totally get that now.

Just last week my friend Jen, who has Stage 4 breast cancer, celebrated her forty-fourth birthday, and it was such a milestone because I'm not sure any of us knew she would get there. When you come face-to-face with mortality and how fleeting all of this really is, there is such an overwhelming sense of gratitude for every single moment, an appreciation for the gift of picking up your kids from car pool, having friends at work that you enjoy, sipping the perfect cup of coffee by the fire on a cold winter day.

By the time you're in your forties, you have experienced a lot of the best and worst life will throw your way, and that takes the sting out of having a few more "laugh lines" and knees that sometimes choose to do their own thing when you get out of bed in the morning.

So far, my forties are about helping Caroline through her pre-teen and teenage years, following where God leads, buying a lot of wrinkle cream with Retinol, taking multiple vitamin supplements in an attempt to hold back the hands of time, making sure I exercise on occasion so I can still move in ten years, and just generally being so much more comfortable in my own skin. I don't worry as much about what people think, or who they want me to be, or what everyone else is doing. There's an ease to life as I sit back and go, "Okay, so this is what I've got to work with." I've figured out how to make peace with what isn't optimal and embrace the parts that make me so grateful.

I read a quote by Max Lucado a while back that says, "The difference between mercy and grace? Mercy gave the prodigal son a second chance. Grace gave him a feast." I feel like when I turned twenty, and later thirty, I'd accepted God's mercy and was so thankful that he'd saved me from myself and a steady stream of bad decisions. But it was in the next decade, my forties, when God showed me what grace really looks like. Because when I look at life, even with all the ups and downs and good and bad and things that haven't turned out the way I wanted, I realize he has blessed me with so much more than I could have imagined. My friends, my family, Perry, and my baby girl. He has given me a feast. So maybe these next decades are about the feast.

Best of all, it's the kind you can enjoy in spite of a declining metabolism.

8

Bangs, Bangs,
You're Dead

A woman who cuts her hair is about to change her life.

Coco Chanel

S everal years ago, I had "the talk" with Caroline. I wasn't really ready for it, but she asked, and I have always done my best to answer her questions honestly and sincerely. And by "the talk," I'm assuming you realize I mean she asked me if I thought she should get bangs.

As a mother, you're never really prepared for these moments.

It was right before the end of the school year, and I explained to her that summer is a bad time to get bangs because we're at the pool almost every day, and also, we live in Texas. No one lives in Texas because they believe the hot and humid summers are great for their hairstyling regimen. We endure the summers because of the Mexican food. The end. I told her that even Kate Middleton regretted cutting bangs, and she has hair that was clearly handwoven by fairies.

Yet Caroline was skeptical about my reasoning and seemed

more than a little unsympathetic to my own horror stories of bangs gone wrong, so I did what a good mother who values her sanity should do and took matters into my own hands by texting my hairdresser the morning of Caroline's appointment to beg her to talk Caroline out of bangs.

We left the stylist later that day with what I felt was a compromise I could live with: long bangs that could be swept to the side and easily pinned back into a ponytail. Caroline complained about them all summer long. And you know what I complained about? My ears. Because they were so tired of listening to her complaining about what I'd begged her not to do. After all that drama and the whole growing-out process that followed, I naively assumed that the matter of bangs had been forever put to rest.

As with many things concerning parenting a pre-teen, I could not have been more wrong.

At the end of the summer, I scheduled a back-to-school haircut for Caroline. All the chlorine and a general lack of hairbrush use had left her hair with a look that most closely resembled a coiffure favored by yetis and reggae singers everywhere. As soon as I told her she had a hair appointment, she immediately launched into stating all the pros and cons of bangs but leaning heavily toward the pro side.

The way Caroline saw it, her previous side bangs really fulfilled no real bang function. They were merely a nuisance that added nothing to her overall look. I kind of wanted to tell her that it was largely due to any lack of styling technique or hairdryer use on her part, but decided against it. It was time to let her take ownership of her hair victories and/or mistakes. It's a rite of passage for all girls. And I say this as a woman who thought it was a good idea in ninth grade to have the right side of my hair cut significantly shorter than the left side to create a swooping effect that found its way back to the permed hair at the back of my head. I have tasted the bitter fruit of hair regret, and it smells a lot like the aforementioned Aussie Sprunch Spray and Final Net. (I wish I could show you the photo documentation of that particular hairstyle captured forever in some fine Olan Mills portraiture. I'm just a girl with a popped collar and a sassy Esprit sweater lounging casually on an enormous wicker chair. As one does.)

As we walked into the beauty salon that day, Caroline was still going back and forth. She wanted my opinion because it always helps her to know what I think so she can ignore it or do the opposite, but I wasn't biting. I told her she would be beautiful no matter what she decided and that bangs can always grow out. There is no hair decision that can't eventually be undone with tears, patience, and hard work. Says the girl who once had a mullet.

She sat in the chair and informed our hair stylist that she wanted bangs. Real bangs. Straight-across bangs that fell across her forehead. Thirty minutes later that's exactly what she had. She spent the rest of the afternoon admiring those bangs, and I don't know that she's ever loved herself more.

Until the next morning when she realized, as most women have, that bangs require some effort. And so she undertook the time-honored ritual of women everywhere and began growing out her brand-new bangs that very day.

I bought her plenty of bobby pins and hair clips and taught her all the tricks for bang transition because I have been there myself countless times. There is a picture of me at about three years old, and I have long hair and the best bangs you've ever seen. I blame this photo of myself and Reese Witherspoon circa 2010 for my eternal bang optimism. I repeatedly forget that I developed a cowlick at some point in my life that really rules out my ability to be my best bang self, yet this still didn't keep me from getting bangs cut the week before I married Perry. To this day he contends he hardly recognized the girl with bangs walking toward him down the aisle because I hadn't had bangs ever in our two years of dating. As much as I ended up regretting that decision, it hasn't kept me from repeating it countless times since then. I eventually made my beloved hairdresser vow that she would never cut my bangs again no matter how much I might plead, or how many pictures of Reese Witherspoon I show her, or whatever hormonal state I am currently in. As sad as I was for Duchess Kate when she had to awkwardly and publicly grow out the bangs she cut shortly after having Princess Charlotte, it validated the fact that truly, no woman is immune from an irrational hair moment where the bangs and grass appear to be greener on the other side. I'd like to think Kate was in the throes of postpartum hormones and grabbed a pair of scissors herself, thinking, "I'll just trim them a bit!" but even though *US Weekly* reminds us often that "Stars, They're Just Like Us!" I'm not sure it completely applies to royalty, who can probably just summon in the royal hairdresser to do as they say. "Give me bangs or off with your head!"

The bangs aren't my only beauty mistake. Years ago I decided to make a lifelong dream come true and purchase a laser hair removal package. I did some research in the form of asking Deidre, a former coworker, about the process. She is an authority on all beauty-type issues, and I knew she had laser hair removal done a few years prior. I called Deidre's laser girl (not the technical term), purchased a hair removal package over the phone because it was ON SALE, and then scheduled the first of my five appointments, which is how many times it takes to completely shock all your hair follicles out of existence.

The day of my first session, I drove to the doctor's office full of excitement at all the possibilities of a life that doesn't require shaving my underarms. I was almost there when Deidre called to check on me. I asked her the question that, in my infinite foolishness, I had neglected to ask earlier: "Does it hurt?" She answered, "Not really. I mean you've had a baby, so you can handle it." Which is never exactly the point on the pain spectrum that I find preferable. I prefer to always be closer to the hangnail end of the spectrum because, yes, I have experienced childbirth, but please note that I only have one child. While it was an incredible experience, it's not one that I'm looking to repeat with any frequency. Plus, I was pretty sure the cost of laser hair removal didn't include an epidural or even a martini.

I went in and signed a stack of paperwork that basically said I could experience a myriad of unpleasant side effects, including the darkening and/or lightening of the skin on my upper lip, neither of which sounds optimal. The dermatologist came in for a consultation, looked at my lip, and stated the obvious "You have dark hair," and then pronounced me a fit candidate for the procedure. Then, Laser Girl walked in and I asked her if it was going to hurt. She nonchalantly replied, "Oh, yeah. It will hurt," and then repeated Deidre's comparison. "But you've had a baby."

Great.

I am an idiot who doesn't ask the right questions far enough in advance. Maybe while I was feeling so giddy about my 20 percent discount for scheduling all five sessions up front, I should have asked about the pain. But oh no, it was much more important that I was getting a good deal. Laser Girl applied some type of gel to my lip and an ice pack and went to work. Ironically, the laser was called the Cool Touch 1000, which is the biggest oxymoron of all time. The Cool Touch 1000 burned like the heat of 10,000 white hot suns surrounding a planet of volcanoes filled with molten lava that has been set on fire. At one point, Laser Girl stopped before moving on to my underarms, and I asked her if someone had burned some popcorn in the office. She replied, "Oh no, that burning smell is your skin and your hair." Well, what a relief. It was just like childbirth but with the smell of burning hair. All I really know about torture is what I learned from *Alias*, but make no mistake about it, this laser hair removal stuff ranks up there for sure. It would make Jack Bauer talk. However, for the following few weeks, I marveled over the fact that I didn't have to shave my underarms or wax my upper lip, and I decided it was all worth it. Like childbirth, the end product is so great that you forget what you endured to get to that point. Unfortunately, unlike childbirth, I was supposed to go back for four more sessions before the process was completely finished.

I decided to be proactive and ask if there was anything I could use to numb the pain before my next session. The nurse told me she could sell me a topical anesthetic that would numb the areas where they would be using the laser. This sounded like an optimal solution, so I slathered that anesthetic both under my arms and on my upper lip. But something in my brain forgot to remember that perhaps I shouldn't lick my lips while there is a thick layer of anesthetic on them. And that's how the pain relief cream did not do one thing to ease the torture under my arms, but left my mouth and throat completely numb for the next twelve hours. So you can jump to the safe conclusion that I still have to shave my underarms and wax my upper lip because I never dared to go back for the remaining three sessions, proving that, for me, pain trumps vanity and convenience.

And that's why I decided the best beauty solution is to just embrace the natural version of yourself.

I'm sorry. I can't even go down that trail like I'm serious. What I've actually concluded is that I prefer my beauty to not involve bangs or laser hair removal, both of which can leave scars, whether they be physical or emotional.

Here's what I do believe in: some good hair products.

Caroline's favorite lazy activity these days is to look around on Pinterest. I know this because many of our school mornings are now like an exam at a beauty school where she rushes into the kitchen three minutes before we need to walk out the door and asks, "Mom, can you do my hair in a messy triple Dutch braid like this one on Pinterest?" as she shows me a braid that would make Princess Elsa claw her eyes out in jealousy and never be able to let it go.

Right. Like if I had that kind of hair styling ability, I would be walking around with this bun on top of my head 99 percent of the time.

I have some hair skills. I can curl or straighten hair like it's my job. I can do a simple French braid. I can do a ponytail and even tease the crown to give it some body. But I am not a magician. I cannot turn fine hair that's been slept on wet and treated to absolutely zero products into a Dutch-braided masterpiece. Not even (insert famous Dutch person here) could do that.

I told Caroline exactly that one day after she asked me to do something "cool" with her hair. I explained it would be really hard to do and she asked, "Why?" and I replied, "Because you have no product in your hair."

She looked right at me and implored, "WHY DOES IT ALWAYS COME BACK TO PRODUCT WITH YOU?"

To which I replied, "Because it always comes back to product."

And that in itself is a valuable lesson. Life always comes back to the right hair products. And not cutting your bangs on a whim.

And never getting laser hair removal.

Unless it includes an epidural.

9

So You Think You Can Parent

Finish each day and be done with it. You have done
what you could. Some blunders and absurdities crept
in; forget them as soon as you can. Tomorrow is a new
day; begin it well and serenely and with too high a spirit
to be encumbered with your old nonsense.

Ralph Waldo Emerson, *Inspiration and Wisdom
from the Pen of Ralph Waldo Emerson*

Let's be honest. Most of us have no clue what we're doing when it comes to parenting our kids; otherwise, why would there be so many articles on Facebook telling us all the ways we are doing it wrong?

I was so much wiser about parenting before I actually had a child, and now most days feel a little like, "Um, I think this is right?" We want to be great at it and have all the right answers and give our kids all the things they need to ensure they don't end up living in a van down by the river, but we don't always know what those things are, and—here's the tricky part—every new stage requires a new set of skills. Just when you think you are really amazing because you taught a small human how to use the toilet, the game changes and the potty-training portion of parenting is just a distant memory with some lingering PTSD.

I currently find myself in the parenting stage of having an adolescent. Anyone else spend their own years as an adolescent reading James Dobson's book *Preparing for Adolescence* because your mom handed it to you and said it would help with any questions you had? I don't remember getting much out of it back then, but now I'm wondering if I should re-read it to help me navigate the world of social politics in junior high for the second time. As if it wasn't painful enough the first time, you have to do it again with a person you love even more than you love yourself. This can lead to fantasizing about yanking a thirteen-year-old girl by the ponytail and telling her to straighten up and act right.

Sometimes that girl is your own child.

Just a few nights ago, Caroline and I were sitting together on the couch when I saw a roach run across the living room floor. I immediately jumped up and began scrambling to kill it with my shoe. This is absolutely the grossest thing ever but far preferable to having a live roach in your house. So I dashed around the living room until I finally got it and then realized Caroline had never even looked up from her iPad.

I asked, "Did you not see me trying to kill that roach?" and she replied, "Oh, is that what you were doing? I just thought you were dancing around the living room acting weird." This basically sums up the daily humiliation of having a teenager. You lose all semblance of coolness and just become someone (in their minds) who's likely to decide to "dance around and act weird" in your living room at midnight.

As a parent, I have made mistakes and will continue to make mistakes. I've been too strict and I've been too lenient. I've yelled too much and I haven't yelled enough. I've second-guessed decisions Perry and I have made, and ultimately find myself on my knees asking God to cover the places where we are going to get it wrong. Parenting is like a pop quiz some days and—SURPRISE!—there's an essay portion at the end.

It's mentally exhausting to navigate all the emotions and the line between being sympathetic and telling them to buck up and quit feeling sorry for themselves. It's determining the line between appropriate amounts of social media and being a Quaker. Or is it the Amish? Who doesn't use computers? I can't remember because I used all my brain power today trying to explain to a thirteen-year-old why it's important to take Spanish as an elective as opposed to being an Office Aide.

For a long time, Caroline was the only kid on the planet who didn't have her own phone. (It's totally true. Just ask her.) EVERYONE had a phone except for her because we are actively looking for ways to ruin her life. We kept telling her she did have a phone; it's called a "home phone" that people can call and talk to her whenever they want. But apparently we've raised a generation of kids who don't get the concept of using a phone to actually talk on it. For them, a phone's primary purpose is to send seventy-four emojis in a row and maybe a selfie that looks like you have a rainbow coming out of your mouth. It's all super similar to how the Greatest Generation stormed the beaches of Normandy during World War II.

Anyway, I decided that since Caroline now had her own phone, we might as well use that power for good, so I installed an app called Locate 360. This app connects her phone to my phone, and I can basically find her location at any given time. At this current phase, it's not all that necessary because either Perry or I drive her just about everywhere she goes, but my thought is that it's like putting a frog in boiling water. We'll condition her now so that, as she has more freedom, she'll be totally used to the fact that we can and will monitor her whereabouts.

You need to know that I was inordinately pleased with myself for installing this app and putting in various alerts to let me know when she arrives at school or when she leaves school or when she walks in our back door. Well, at least until I had a text exchange with her while she was at school that went like this:

> **Caroline:** Mom, did you install something called Locate 360 on my phone?
>
> **Me:** Yes, I did! Love you!
>
> **Caroline:** Okay, because it alerted me to tell me you left the house and went to get a pedicure. I can totally stalk you during the day now!

So. Um. That's not really how it was supposed to go down. Mainly because it blows my whole elaborate scheme that I work really hard all day long while she's at school. Pop quiz FAIL for the day.

The thing is, I don't know that any other generation of parents has worried about their kids the way we do. I think it's partly because social media has made us so aware of every little thing that can go wrong. All it takes is a quick scan of your Facebook newsfeed to find a story about a kid who drowned hours after leaving the pool, or a teenager who was in a car wreck because he was texting and driving, or that we need to cherish every moment with our kids and never tell them to hurry up, or that we can't make our kids the center of our universe because they will become narcissists who can't function in society. If we're not overwhelmed by all the things that can go wrong, we will be by all the ways we're falling short. All it takes is one quick look at Instagram to see all the moms who are doing it better. They do things like play board games and have hot chocolate bars waiting for their kids when they get home from school and pack healthy lunches in Bento boxes with sandwiches cut in the shape of R2-D2. Or maybe they just take pictures to make it look that way. We'll never know for sure. But the pressure to do it all perfectly is stifling, and honestly, I don't think it's doing us—or our kids—any favors. We can't prepare them for the real world if we're constantly protecting them from the real world. We can't teach them to be brave if all they see from us is that we are scared. They'll never learn that having sandwiches that look like Star Wars characters isn't really a thing if we keep carving those light sabers out of cauliflower.

The bottom line is, life is going to come with hard times, disappointments, challenges, and all those other things that we all know deep down are the very things that end up shaping our character.

A few months ago, a high school student in our community committed suicide after being continually bullied by a group of fellow students. From what I know, the majority of this took place over various social media channels, and I won't even pretend I know all the ways there are these days to harass someone online. I thought I was so tech savvy because I know kids create Finstagram accounts (that's a fake Instagram) and use Snapchat, but in the days that followed this tragedy, I read about so many other apps that make cyber-bullying easier than ever.

I watched our community grapple with what should have been done differently, what could have been done differently, and what we need to do to keep our kids from being bullied or being a bully. Spoiler alert: I don't know all the answers to these questions. In fact, at one of my speaking events last year, someone introduced me as "a comedian and a parenting expert," and I cringed because I'm not a comedian (as evidenced by the fact that no one has ever followed something I've said with a ba-da-bum on the drums) and I am certainly no parenting expert, seeing as how I'm only twelve-and-a-half years into this job.

But here are a few things I do know. I know the darkness wants to come for our kids. I know that evil is everywhere and looking for a chance to whisper to them that they are less than, that they're inadequate, that they'll never be enough, and that their lives don't matter. I know that bullying has gone on from the beginning of time and has never been easier now that we can hide behind a keyboard and show our rear ends without showing our faces. I know that many people are more fragile than they appear, and we need to treat our fellow human beings with kindness and respect even and perhaps especially when they are different from us and we don't agree with them. And I know our kids are looking to us to model appropriate behavior. They may not act like it or acknowledge it, but they know better than anyone if who we are in public is the same as who we are in private.

What if we teach our kids that their true identity and security is found in the fact that they "are God's handiwork, created in Christ Jesus to do good works, which God prepared in advance for [them] to do" (Ephesians 2:10)? Each of us is fearfully and wonderfully made, and God has put us in our families, schools, communities, and the world in this time and in this generation for a very specific and unique reason. And instead of finding power or making ourselves feel better by making someone else feel small and insignificant, we will never feel more empowered or confident than when we run our own race to discover the purpose for which God created us.

What if we showed our kids what kindness and compassion look like? There is never any weakness in showing mercy and grace, because those characteristics are the very heartbeat of God. Let's live in a way that teaches our children the importance of loving our neighbors and that peers aren't our competition. When we begin to see our own value, we realize that no one else's successes or accomplishments diminish our own but rather we see that God has a unique path for each of us. Sometimes a closed door is the very thing that leads us to our calling. We can walk our road without worrying if someone else's road looks better. The comparison trap is an endless vortex of nothingness that serves only to make us feel insecure and discontented because we are measuring our insides against someone else's outside.

What if we instill in our kids the words of the apostle Paul to young Timothy, "For God has not given us a spirit of fear, but of power and of love and of a sound mind" (2 Timothy 1:7 NKJV)? God doesn't want us to live in fear. We can call on his power and love to stand up to the bullies in this world and, maybe even more importantly, to speak up for those who are too broken and have been hurt too badly to defend themselves. A famous quote by philosopher Edmund Burke says, "The only thing necessary for the triumph of evil is for good men to do nothing." Let's raise good men and women who aren't afraid to speak up or do something when they see wrong.

There is so much emphasis on paying attention to what our

kids see online, what apps they use on their phones, who they hang out with at school and in their free time—and all those things are important. I absolutely check Caroline's phone on a regular basis and will continue to as long as I'm paying for it. And I will flat out take it away from her if I ever see that she's not using it like a responsible member of society. Our mantra here is "Social media is a privilege, not a right," and I plan to say it over and over again, and any eye rolling will only make me say it more, maybe even have a T-shirt made and turn it into a quote with a flowery border that I post on Instagram.

But I think I'm realizing the most important thing to teach her is to be true to herself and who we are raising her to be—even when we're not looking, even when she's not at school, and even when no one will know what she did—because one of these days she'll be on her own and will need to decide these things for herself. In the meantime, we monitor, we discuss, and we discipline if something seems amiss.

The Bible says, "Point your kids in the right direction—when they're old they won't be lost" (Proverbs 22:6 MSG), which means it's our job to give them what is basically a road map for life. It takes work and perseverance and dedication to raise our kids. It takes sacrifice and commitment and dying to self as we spend eighteen short—let's be honest LIGHTNING FAST—years pouring into them and equipping them to be responsible, productive, kind, and ideally, employed adults. And make no mistake; our kids will model what they see much more than what we say.

The thought that keeps running through my mind and heart since that precious young man took his own life is that we are called to be the light of the world, a city on a hill. In the days when Jesus spoke those words, a city lit up on a hill would have been a haven for weary travelers, a welcome sight and an indication that they were nearing a good meal and a warm bed to sustain them for the rest of their journey. I want our kids to be a city on a hill, a safe harbor for those who need refuge in the midst of life's storms. The only way I know to accomplish that is to allow the love of Christ to take hold of our hearts and the hearts of our children so that we can show each other how to find a way home when we are lost, to hold out hope when we see someone is hurting, and to celebrate how our differences enable each of us to shine our own unique ray of light in the midst of a dark night.

Small Things

Things I Wish I'd Known When I Became a Mom

And should she choose to be a Mother one day, be my eyes, Lord, that I may see her, lying on a blanket on the floor at 4:50 a.m., all-at-once exhausted, bored, and in love with the little creature whose poop is leaking up its back.

"My mother did this for me once," she will realize as she cleans feces off her baby's neck. "My mother did this for me." And the delayed gratitude will wash over her as it does each generation and she will make a Mental Note to call me. And she will forget. But I'll know, because I peeped it with Your God eyes.

Tina Fey, *Bossypants*

107

For about the first six weeks of Caroline's life, I was convinced that motherhood was all part of a vast conspiracy by women everywhere, who were already mothers, to make the rest of us as sleep deprived as they were. It wasn't that I didn't love her more than I ever knew I could love anything, but nothing prepares you for how hard it is and how ill-prepared you are for the following eighteen or so years that they'll live under your roof.

If I could go back in time, here are a few things I'd tell my new-mom self.

1. I know you're freaked out because the hospital just let you walk out of there with a baby and you're an idiot. But riding in the backseat to monitor every single movement she makes on the way home isn't really necessary.
2. Don't throw away that gigantic pacifier the hospital sent home with you, because it turns out that's the only one she'll like for the first six months of her life.
3. Breastfeeding is great when it works, but nobody is going to end up in long-term therapy just because they drank formula from a bottle.
4. At some point, you will be able to watch a movie that has more violence or tragedy than *Little Women* without feeling like you need to wrap your entire home in bubble wrap to protect you and your child from the cold, cruel world.
5. It's okay that all you accomplished today was brushing your teeth. Embrace the victory. In fact, celebrate it with a glass of wine or a pint of ice cream.
6. The stains newborn yellow poop leaves behind aren't ever going to come out, so go rock your baby and quit wasting your time attempting the impossible.

7. Kids all reach their milestones in their own time. Trying to force your two-week-old to hold a rattle isn't going to increase her chances of participating in the Olympics someday. Although it may increase the odds that she'll need therapy.
8. Toddlers can be the worst. Don't take it personally. It's them, not you.
9. Potty training is terrible for everyone. Don't listen to your friend who tells you her child couldn't wait to poop on the potty. She's a liar. Kids think their poop is part of their soul and hate to flush it away.
10. You will be so grateful you didn't listen to the woman who advised you to shave your child's head when she was a year old because it allegedly ensures she will have thick hair as she gets older.
11. Never underestimate the power of a well-timed bribe. It's okay because everyone does it. A bag of M&Ms can be a powerful tool if used wisely.
12. Someday, many years later, you will still, oddly enough, remember every word of the theme song to *Mickey Mouse Clubhouse* even though you wrote a check yesterday and started to write the year with 19 before you realized, *Oh, right, it's been a new century for almost two decades.*
13. On a similar note, you won't believe you devoted so much time to *The Wiggles*, particularly Captain Feathersword. I mean, what the heck?
14. It's okay to lock yourself in the bathroom for a few minutes. Sometimes even mommies need a time out.
15. There will come a day when you will not have to chase that chubby toddler around the pool while you're wearing a swimsuit. In fact, you'll be able to sit poolside and read a magazine while they swim.

16. But the truth is, you'll be a little sad that those days are gone, so try to enjoy them while they last. Even when you have to make the walk of shame with a child wearing a swim diaper that has gone awry due to an overflow of feces, thanks to the effects of your kid ingesting too much chlorine and flimsy elastic at the legs.

17. Don't kill yourself taking the kid to the zoo. Why does everyone assume kids want to see animals stand around in the hot sun all the time? I have a theory it's just propaganda developed by zoo investors.

18. Once school starts, your child will grow up like a freight train going down the tracks. It is wonderful and magical and heartbreaking and exhilarating and nerve-wracking and like one big punch in the gut all at the same time.

19. Volunteer in the classroom as much as you can during elementary school because they will want you to make yourself scarce in their school environment by junior high.

20. I know it doesn't feel like it when you're exhausted and drained and just had to chase a toddler through the grocery store, but it goes by in a blink. A BLINK. Try to enjoy it as much as you can, and drink a glass of wine on the days you just can't even.

10

Fish, Frogs, Crabs, and a Farm of Lies

We are never owning another fish.

Melanie Shankle

My mother-in-law stopped by the other day to bring Caroline a little Easter basket she'd put together for her. It was about three days before Easter, but this is the kind of woman my mother-in-law is. She invariably shows up—sometimes at least a week early—for any life occasion with a thoughtful gift that she no doubt purchased several months prior. She routinely gifts things that are monogrammed because she is a person who plans far enough in advance to actually have time to get things monogrammed without having to pay a $20 rush fee to get it finished in time. She also emails me no later than early September every year to see what Caroline might like for Christmas.

This is who I want to be.

In reality, I am a person who only remembers major holidays because everyone else in the world is celebrating them on the same day. And even with all the seasonal aisles at Target screaming at me to be a better person, my daughter knows what it's like to trick-or-treat carrying a plastic grocery bag from HEB or to have a decorative basket I use around the house suddenly be confiscated by the Easter Bunny to fill with eggs and chocolate bunnies. I always vow to be better next time. Next year will be the year we make those hollow rolls I see on Pinterest so we can totally comprehend the resurrection of Christ using baked goods! This Christmas will be the time our Elf on the Shelf finally quits being a slacker and learns to zip line on dental floss with all the Barbie dolls and ride in a Jeep with G.I. Joe and take a bath in marshmallows!

As for birthdays, I need you to know that my inability to remember your birthday is no indication of my love for you. Facebook and iPhones have helped me immensely with this, yet I still manage to end up buying a gift or card on the day of the event. Or—let's be honest—the day after. To my shame and horror, I've managed to forget my mother-in-law's birthday two years in a row. Even worse, she couldn't be sweeter or more understanding about it. She even gives me an out by saying I'm an artist and it's just not the way my brain works. And she's right. I *am* an artist, provided your definition of an artist is some-one who sits around trying to type words on a computer while looking more like someone who is recovering from a prolonged illness, has no access to a hairbrush, and has been left with only a pair of cropped sweatpants and a T-shirt that reads "Aggie Baseball 1994." Because why update my T-shirt collection to the current century?

Anyway, back to my mother-in-law delivering the Easter basket, which was never even the real point of this story (I'm off in the weeds looking for a squirrel). She stayed to visit for a while, and we sat out in the backyard while Caroline juggled her soccer ball before deciding to catch a lizard that was climbing up the side of our house. My mother-in-law told her to turn it over and stroke its belly, because apparently she is a woman of many talents and knows that lizards like that. I personally wouldn't know what lizards like because I believe they are just snakes with legs and avoid them at all costs, maybe while also screaming, "GET IT AWAY! GET IT AWAY!"

The stomach rubbing must have worked, because the lizard decided it liked Caroline and just stayed on her arm even after she let it go. This caused my mother-in-law to remember that when she was a girl, you used to be able to buy a lizard with a collar and a chain that you could attach to your shirt at the county fair. This is really more than I can process and brings up so, so many questions. Who catches the lizards? How do you get a collar on them? Where was PETA when this whole thing was going down? Even Caroline agreed, because she told Perry about it later at dinner that night and said, "That just kind of seems like animal cruelty." Which I felt was supremely ironic coming from someone who once took three weeks to notice her pet goldfish had died and been flushed away to the big aquarium in the sky. Or the sewer. Depending on your beliefs concerning the viability of a fish afterlife.

In fact, it was her particular lack of concern for fish life that led me to issue my ultimatum before each ensuing school carnival that Caroline was under no circumstances to play a game wherein a goldfish in a plastic bag was the prize. I don't know what genius originally decided that giving elementary-school-aged children a fish in a plastic baggie sealed with a rubber band was a good idea, but I now have my suspicions that they were a descendant of whomever put those collars on lizards. In my experience, the goldfish prize is a losing proposition either way. You either end up with an overly tired and dramatic child mourning the loss of her beloved pet of one hour, an hour she spent jostling said pet in a hostile environment that included a round of musical chairs, a cakewalk, and a trip on a bounce castle. Or you have yourself a "free" pet goldfish who will require a bowl, a plastic treasure chest full of fake treasure, colored rocks, and fish flakes. Because make no mistake, pets that come into your home are going to be your responsibility no matter how many promises a child makes to the contrary. Children are filthy liars at worst and con artists at best.

My precious child outsmarted me, though, because the year after my no goldfish stance, she obeyed me and played a carnival game where she won a hermit crab. A hermit crab she christened Phillip. Which seemed like an incredibly regal name for something with antennae that eats freeze-dried shrimp.

Perry and I tried to make a temporary habitat for Phillip. Or as people in the crab business call it, a CRABITAT. He spent the night in one of my glass mixing bowls (which went in the trash immediately afterwards) with the lid of a spice jar as a water dish and only a layer of sand and the memories of his time at the pet shop with his old crab friends to keep him warm. We went to bed that night with the satisfaction that only comes with the knowledge you now own a hermit crab, and the next day we went to the pet store, where we spent forty American dollars gathering everything we needed to keep our FREE hermit crab in the style to which he apparently had grown accustomed.

Oh, and Caroline also talked me into buying a friend for Phillip. She named her Clementine. A month after that, we decided the more the merrier in our little crabitat and added Big Daddy. Which means you can just call me sucker.

Six months later, I decided it was time to get rid of Caroline's hermit crabs and their accompanying crabitat. Normally, I might have felt guilty about this, but Phillip had died almost three months prior and it took her every bit of two and a half months to even notice. However, we were left with Big Daddy and Clementine, and I wasn't sure what you do with unwanted crabs (all of a sudden this sounds like an unfortunate late-night infomercial) and didn't feel like I could just throw them away. The truth is they were stinking up my house with all their freeze-dried shrimp food, and it was time to bid them adieu. So I did what I do in all complicated situations: I set the crabitat with the crabs outside on the back porch and told Perry to handle it.

For some reason, he decided to put Clementine and Big Daddy in the dog's water bucket to let them have one last swim or something. I don't know. Then his phone rang, and he forgot about them and left for his family's ranch. All I know is I looked outside hours later and noticed the dog was acting weird about drinking water. When I went to investigate, there were Big Daddy and Clementine swimming happily in the water dish. Heaven knows it's probably the only water they'd had in weeks, since Caroline had proven to be the crab-version of Dr. Kevorkian.

As I was removing the crabs from the dog's water dish, Caroline started to walk outside. I didn't want her to see the crabs and be reminded of their existence, so I hurriedly set them down behind it and went inside. When I finally remembered what I'd done hours later, I discovered they were nowhere to be found. They made a mass crab exodus. If you consider two crabs to constitute a mass exodus. I do, because in any economy, two crabs are really two crabs too many to have roaming freely in your backyard. I like to think maybe they packed their teeny tiny crab bags and left our house for good; that they were like little crab Joads in search of a better life. Either that or they were eaten by the dog.

A few years later Caroline began junior high, and I breathed a sigh of relief that the fish-and-crab-winning days of elementary school were behind us forever. But I went out of town one weekend and something developed while I was away.

I knew Perry and Caroline had plans to go to the ranch after I left town, but nothing prepared me for what she told me when I called home to check on them late Saturday night. I asked, "Did you have a great day? How was the ranch?" and she excitely replied, "Yes! We had a great time! Dad let me bring home five hundred tadpoles!"

Umm.

When did my husband decide to see how many tadpoles it takes before I check myself into a home?

The answer to that word problem is that five hundred tadpoles are significantly more than the number of tadpoles I am equipped to handle, which is zero. What little I understand about basic biology was enough for me to know our backyard was about to look like a plague from the days of Moses and Pharaoh. Which meant I'd have to move.

Caroline wanted to show me her new "pets" first thing when I got back home, and there they were swimming around in what used to be a container for food storage and therefore caused me to reject all plastic storage apparatuses for the rest of eternity. I put a picture of all the tadpoles swimming around a big piece of wood on Instagram later that day and someone commented that they thought it was meat I had marinating for dinner, and that is why I am now a vegetarian.

(I'm not really a vegetarian. But I could be. Except for the hamburgers. And the chicken fried steak.)

I immediately noticed that some of the tadpoles, much like Bruce Jenner in 2015, had begun to transition into something else. I may even have seen what I believed to be tiny hopping motions, but I couldn't process that any further or FOR SALE SIGN IN MY FRONT YARD. Caroline explained she was hoping to sell some of them to her classmates in a business proposition I can only assume was making me extremely popular among my fellow mothers. But she didn't have many takers. I think she said about three people were interested. Which left us at about four hundred and ninety-seven tadpoles that were going to need to be relocated to a neighborhood that wasn't my backyard. So the rest of that week was spent monitoring the real, live biology lab happening on our back porch while attempting to convince Caroline that if you love something, you need to set it free. Sting told us that years ago, and he is rarely wrong. He also told us De Do Do Do, De Da Da Da, but that didn't really apply to the situation at hand, so I stuck with free, free, set them free. I just happened to know the perfect creek nearby, where we could show the tadpoles how much we loved them. They didn't come back, so clearly they weren't really ours to begin with.

You'd think that would be the definitive end of our taking in any pet that wasn't a dog, but you are giving me way too much credit. It continued at Christmas when Gulley and her boys, Will and Jackson, gave Caroline an ant farm. I agreed to this gift because it was one of those green gel ant farms that allegedly required nothing of you except being bored enough to watch ants dig tunnels. I was also powerless to tell Gulley not to buy Caroline an ant farm since I'd recently helped Gulley's youngest son, Will, convince her to buy him a bearded dragon and had maybe even used the phrase, "It's the Golden Retriever of the lizard world!"

We went online a few days later to order our supply of ants because the alternative was to find our own out in the yard or something, and let me just say AS IF. The confirmation email let us know that our ants would arrive in approximately two to three weeks depending on the weather in our area, because it can't be too hot or too cold or the ants might die in transport. Apparently being in transit with the US Postal Service is harsher than living out in nature.

However, I found myself on the horns of a dilemma when the ants arrived because the package said the ants needed to be placed in their new home IMMEDIATELY and Caroline was at the ranch for the day with Perry. I knew they wouldn't be home until much later that night. So the sole burden of placing the ants fell squarely on my shoulders. I later learned I could have waited and IMMEDIATELY didn't so much mean IMMEDIATELY as it meant just sometime in the next twelve or so hours. But it's too late now. (Dear Ant Suppliers, please don't use the word IMMEDIATELY if you don't mean it. It's very alarming.)

I carefully read all the instructions to make sure I did everything the way it was supposed to be done to ensure our ants' safe arrival in their new home. The first step was to poke three holes in the gel farm, which I guess helps them get started in their new environment. The second step was to place the test tube full of ants into the refrigerator for fifteen minutes so they'd be lethargic when I dumped them in and thus not as likely to try to escape from gel Alcatraz, so I finished folding some laundry and straightening up the house while the ants chilled in the fridge. I mean that literally. Although maybe they found the Pinot Grigio I keep on hand and chilled both literally and figuratively. I don't know an ant's life.

After fifteen or maybe thirty minutes (I lost track of time. Get off my back.), I opened the top of the ant farm and dumped all the ants into their new home with fear and trembling. And, well, the scene was exactly what you'd expect. Ants everywhere. Ants milling and crawling and trying desperately to find a way to escape their new gel-filled enclosure.

I spent the rest of the afternoon checking on the ants' progress, and I was afraid I'd basically killed a bunch of ants because they weren't doing much of anything. Maybe they were stunned. Or maybe it's because they'd been in the fridge longer than necessary. In all fairness, if someone put me in a tube, mailed me, stuck me in an igloo and then dumped me out on a beach somewhere, I'd be a little shell-shocked too. It might take me a day or two to find the will or courage to make a sand castle or to quit rocking back and forth in the fetal position.

But by the time Caroline got home later that night, the ants had begun to dig some tunnels. They'd piled their dead ant friends in a corner (They didn't all make it. Tragic, I know.) and were working furiously in some type of assembly line formation.

It was what I saw the next morning that stopped me in my tracks. It's about to get all *Charlotte's Web* up in here in case you're wondering when this whole drawn-out story about some ants is going to come together, and also when I might quote a DMX song. Because the ants had worked furiously to tunnel out a message in the green gel of the ant farm that clearly spelled out:

LIE

I know. What could it all mean? Did they think I was lying? Were *they* lying? Was their whole life a lie now that they'd been subjected to a life of hard labor on an ant farm? Did the people at Uncle Milton and the US Postal Service tell them they were going to a place with green pastures to roam around and cows to milk while wearing jaunty straw hats and perhaps tiny pairs of overalls?

Then, as if that wasn't enough, I settled in on the couch to go through my email and was immediately greeted by an email in my inbox that began "SALUTATIONS!"

Are you getting this? Do you see that the email said SALUTATIONS? That is exactly how Charlotte greeted Wilbur in *Charlotte's Web*. It was her fancy way of saying hello.

What were the odds that on the same morning the ants wrote LIE, I'd get an email sending "salutations"? And it wasn't a real email. It was a spam email from an unknown address. I can't say for sure, but I think the ants sent it. How else do you explain it?

All I knew was that if I woke up the next morning to find the word RADIANT spelled out in the ant farm, I was either throwing them away or taking them to the county fair.

While I was out running errands several days later, I received a distressing text from Perry. It read, "Caroline's ants are out. Just nuked half of them."

Well. That wasn't good.

I called him and asked, "What do you mean the ants are out? How did that happen? Did you squash them?" He replied, "I'm not sure how they got out, but it looks like the lid wasn't on good and some of them escaped. I sprayed them with Windex."

The good news (if this can be considered good news) was

that only some of them escaped, and Perry and his Windex came to the rescue at just the right time. It was bound to happen. I mean they'd already let me know they felt they were living a lie.

Plus, I think they had changed "LIE" to "LIB" the night before, which I felt might be a political declaration, and if that was the case, then it was no wonder they felt the need to move on from our conservative household, especially considering they might be in need of Obamacare after the Windex incident.

Needless to say, we didn't mention the ant mutiny to Caroline when she got home from school. I wasn't too worried that she'd notice half her ants were missing when you consider that her hermit crabs escaped in our backyard and she never even realized they were gone.

The lesson here is that it's better to stick with dogs if you want pets.

Or maybe even a lizard on a chain.

Also, we should all be more like my mother-in-law and buy thoughtful, meaningful gifts and deliver them in a timely manner.

——————— *Small Things* ———————

Things I Wish I'd Known Before Getting a Hermit Crab as a Pet

1. DON'T.

True Tales of Canine Delinquents

> Dogs are minor angels, and I don't mean that facetiously. They love unconditionally, forgive immediately, are the truest of friends, willing to do anything that makes us happy . . . If we attributed some of those qualities to a person we would say they are special. If they had ALL of them, we would call them angelic.
>
> Jonathan Carroll from *Teaching the Dog to Read*

Several years ago, Caroline and I spent an afternoon watching the movie, *My Dog Skip*. Have you ever seen this movie? It's like the kid version of *Marley & Me* and guaranteed to put you straight in the bed with a full-on ugly cry, particularly if you watch it during a bout of PMS. Ask me how I know.

As we watched it, my mind became overwhelmed with several thoughts. First, I felt that we needed to get Caroline her own puppy immediately. Then I became worried about how sad that hypothetical puppy would be someday when she left for college, and that led me down a road of wondering how I'm going to survive when she leaves for college, because apparently I like to worry about things a decade in advance. But most of all, it made me remember how much I always wanted a dog when I was a kid.

I never had a dog growing up. My mom let us have cats, but a dog was never on the table. While cats have their own charm, kind of like a cross between a cactus and a Care Bear, provided you don't mind being completely ignored by an animal that would rather lick its own rear end repeatedly than pay attention to you, they never fulfilled my dream of having a puppy.

When Perry and I were newlyweds, we decided we were ready to take the next step in our lives as real adults and get a dog. Perry really wanted a Blue Heeler (also known as an Australian Cattle Dog) and I just wanted a puppy! Any puppy! All the puppies are so cute! And so we began to look at litters of puppies. Our search was over as soon as we saw our Scout.

He didn't look like a typical Heeler. His face was much darker, and whereas most Heelers are high-energy and protective, Scout preferred a lap and welcomed everyone into our backyard with a wagging tail. He never acted like a dog. In fact, Perry remarked after a few days of owning him that he'd never had a dog that acted less like a dog than Scout. Of course, it probably didn't help that we bought him from a woman who lived in a trailer home in Hondo, Texas, and she informed us as we were walking out the door with him that he really enjoyed sleeping on her couch and watching "the color TV."

Scout was my first dog, my first experience with something that loved me totally and completely and greeted me with unmatched enthusiasm even if I'd only been gone five minutes. I was crazy about him in that way you are before you have kids, when your dog is your baby. I hated to leave him when I had to go to work in the morning. I rushed home at lunch to see him. I took him to Sonic to get ice cream. Let's put it this way: I SANG HIM LULLABIES while rocking him on my lap. I was besotted.

When he was about three months old, our vet discovered he had a hole in his heart that needed to be closed up or he wouldn't live more than a year. At the time, it was a surgery that could only be done at Texas A&M and wasn't inexpensive, but he was my baby so Perry and I drove him to College Station to have heart surgery that would save his life.

Boy, did we get our money's worth. Scout turned out to be an adrenaline junkie who never stopped. We had to build a higher fence in our backyard because he would get so excited he'd just jump over it. Perry and I would stand at either end of the back-yard and take turns calling him. He'd come barreling at us as fast as he could and leap into our arms. Heaven help the raccoons he managed to chase down at the ranch, because they weren't long for this world.

Scout never met a stranger, and we always said he'd totally sell us out for a hamburger. Turns out, at night he really did like to watch "the color TV." He'd growl at the deer on Perry's hunting shows and then fall asleep while he dreamed of chasing them down, evidenced by the way his paws moved constantly as he slept.

During those first few years, Scout was my original road trip partner. Gulley lived in Austin at the time, and I'd go visit her on weekends when Perry was hunting. I always brought Scout with me. He loved being at Gulley's because he loved her dog, Annie. Plus, we fed him some expensive, healthy food, and Gulley fed Annie something called Dinnertime from HEB. Scout would scarf that food down like a kid at McDonald's and have the worst gas all the way back home to San Antonio. But he and Annie would play non-stop, and Gulley and I declared them to be best friends. They were our first generation of best friends.

A year after we got Scout, we brought home another Heeler we named Jem. Jem couldn't have been more different from Scout and preferred to spend his time outdoors, growling and barking at anyone who came within a twenty-foot radius of our backyard. But both dogs became my constant shadows when I was pregnant with Caroline. Jem even went so far to share my morning sickness (Who am I kidding? It was all-day sickness.) and would throw up any time I threw up. It was one of the hottest summers ever in San Antonio during the last months of my pregnancy, and the three of us would pile up on the couch in the air-conditioning and watch endless episodes of *Alias*. This was in the days before the DVR, so I'm talking about popping in VHS tape after VHS tape in the VCR just like I was a pioneer.

When we brought Caroline home from the hospital, we didn't have to worry about Scout or Jem because they immediately knew she was a part of our pack. They seemed to accept that they had moved down a rung in our family hierarchy but took it in stride. Sadly, Jem had an accident down at the ranch when Caroline was about five months old, and we had to put him to sleep. I can still remember dropping Caroline off at my mother-in-law's house so I could go be with Jem to say good-bye. Scout was the first dog I'd ever owned, but Jem was the first dog I ever lost, and the pain of losing him made me feel like I couldn't breathe. Losing a beloved dog and postpartum hormones are a dreadful cocktail.

About two weeks after that, we got another Heeler named Bruiser. I don't remember one thing about Bruiser's puppy days. I was still in the fog of losing Jem and having a newborn, so basically sheer survival mode. I can't even tell you why we thought it was a good idea to add a puppy to that mix, except that I decided Scout might be lonely without a buddy.

When Scout was a puppy, I came just shy of burping him after he ate and still credit him as being part of what gave me the courage to become a mom to an actual human. But poor Bruiser just had to make do. There were no lullabies. I never rocked him in my lap. I had a baby and spent Bruiser's puppyhood barely treading water. But he was a good dog, loyal to his marrow and always so gentle with Caroline, even as she unwittingly taunted him while she toddled around the backyard holding all manner of animal crackers loosely in her sticky toddler hands.

(I am giving you this illustrious history of "Dogs We Have Owned" because I feel you need to know our dog ownership background. You can reference this section in your two-star review of this book on Amazon and write, "I don't know why she thinks anyone cares about her dogs or wants to hear about them for an entire chapter.")

Anyway, by the time Caroline became old enough to enjoy having a dog and emotionally astute enough to sob her way through the ending of *My Dog Skip*, Scout and Bruiser were old dogs, so she began the time-honored tradition of begging us to buy her a puppy. But we figured it was only a matter of time before Scout or Bruiser passed away, and then we could think about a new puppy because you know how many dogs is too many dogs? More than two.

In fact, Scout had a health scare two years earlier, and the vet told us then that he only had about three to six months left at best. Let me know if that math doesn't add up for you either. Then Bruiser was diagnosed with a degenerative spine and could barely get around anymore. In short, we were running a geriatric facility for dogs in our backyard. Apparently we were doing a heck of a job, because they continued to beat the odds.

So we became more serious about finding a puppy for Caroline, because at the rate Scout and Bruiser were continuing to defy all canine odds, she might be leaving for college before they actually left this world.

Perry found out about a litter of puppies that would be ready soon, but then there was some sort of miscommunication, and we found out they'd already committed all the puppies to other homes, which I just realized makes it sound like they ended up in some type of asylum situation. This was not the case. I'm sure they were loving homes full of Puppy Chow and plenty of stuffed toys to tear up like it's their job.

Anyway, the guy with the first litter put us in touch with a friend of his who also had puppies and GUESS WHAT? They were eight-and-a-half weeks old and ready to go to new homes immediately. We had less than twenty-four hours to get our house puppy-ready. As if that's a real thing. No house can truly be puppy-ready unless it's covered in floor-to-ceiling Teflon and has a closet full of sedatives.

I picked up Caroline from school, we drove to the pet supply store to pick up all the various accouterments a puppy requires, and then we met Perry to go get our puppy. But something un-expected happened when we went to get our girl. She had a sister. Dang those puppy eyes and that puppy breath. It turns even the hardest hearted into someone who baby talks. One minute we were picking up a single puppy, and then we were saying, "So do you want to come up with us, too? Do you want to come live with your sister, precious punkin baby girl? Are you the sweetest girl ever who needs a home?" And that's how we ended up with two Blue Lacys named Piper and Mabel. Little-known fact about Blue Lacys: they are the official state dog of Texas and are often mistaken for small Weimaraners with their blue-gray coat and light eyes. In other words, they were irresistible to me.

Oh, sure. They looked innocent enough. That was part of their master plan. But the first night they were home, they shredded both the lining of my shower curtain and the sea grass rug in our living room. They were two little maniacs who trained us more than we trained them, as evidenced by the fact that we only lasted a week before they were no longer sleeping in their kennels but right next to us in the bedroom. Also, the lush, green grass in our backyard became a distant memory as they dug holes and chased each other all over the place.

But I loved them. I loved their puppy breath and Piper's pretty eyes and the way Mabel put her front paws in the water dish when she drank. I loved the way their ears constantly flopped backward like little superhero capes and how they ran across the yard to meet us at the gate when we pulled up in the driveway. They were precious. Those things are what helped me survive their puppy months and kept me from listing them for sale on Craigslist.

Because there were moments I thought we must have been out of our minds to bring home two creatures with an energy level resembling my KitchenAid mixer's highest setting—well, that is if my mixer also occasionally liked to pee on the rug and chew up flip-flops while racing at full speed around the kitchen.

Here we had finally reached the point where we had a child who could make her own sandwiches and appreciate the fine art of sleeping late, and then we added two poop machines who liked to wake up barking at the crack of dawn. What were they barking at, you ask? Each other, Scout, Bruiser, a dog walking by, a leaf falling from a tree, an ant crawling on the sidewalk, the very air.

And so the daily routine that summer after we first brought home Piper and Mabel was this: I woke up to the dogs barking as soon as Perry leaves for work. They were barking because he had left; they were barking because it's morning; they were barking because they were alive. I'd lie in bed for a few minutes to see if the barking would stop. When it inevitably didn't, I stumbled outside and greeted the puppies, who were jumping up and down like they were on bungee cords hovering over a canyon, with a warm, loving question along the lines of "Why are y'all so dumb?" which was my way of saying, "I love you so much but you are driving me to a point that is a hair shy of a mental institution."

But they had me where they wanted me, which meant I was helpless to resist their little puppy charms and let them in to sit with me while I drank my coffee at a much earlier hour than I really prefer in the summertime. Or ever. They'd curl up near me and take a little morning nap while I did my Bible study and checked Twitter or whatever, and I'd get lulled into thinking they're precious. It reminded me of that episode of *Friends* where Phoebe's brother looks at his sleeping triplets and says, "I really treasure these moments. Because pretty soon they're going to wake up again."

It was usually around that time that one of them would jump down and attack the fireplace tools because the fireplace tools exist and are very menacing sitting there lifelessly on the hearth. Then they'd begin to race around the house, sliding and skidding on the wood floors like kids at a roller rink for the first time, until I opened the back door and called their names, which is when they would go flying outside to annoy Scout and Bruiser. It made me feel like we might as well have brought home two Tasmanian devils.

One of Piper and Mabel's favorite activities is what I like to call "Your Bone Looks Better than Mine." They each have their own bone. They are exactly the same. And they are happy with their respective bones for 1.3 seconds before each feels her bone must be inadequate compared to her sister's bone. If you ever doubt that all living creatures have something innate that makes them feel like someone else might have something better, the puppies were living proof it's true. They'd growl and chase to get each other's bones and then were completely dissatisfied and wanted their original bones back two seconds later.

It was as fun for me as you're imagining. I'd hear myself saying things like "Don't be mean to your sister!" and "Why would you do that to your sister?" and "Sisters don't fight! Sisters love!"

What I'm saying is, I didn't even know who I was anymore.

Then, to add insult to injury, Scout peed on the rug. Scout. Our sixteen-year-old dog who has been house-trained for fifteen-and-a-half years. He just stood there and let it go. Just like Elsa in *Frozen* except he didn't freeze anything; he just urinated. On my antique rug.

So I used my dog psychology skills and asked him, "WHY DID YOU DO THAT? WHY? WHAT IS HAPPENING?" as I escorted him out of the house. Because it's one thing when a baby pees on your rug, but it's an entirely different kettle of fish when Grandpa does it. We can just start with sheer volume and go on from there.

Truth be told, I'd been telling Perry for months that I thought

Scout had dementia, and I felt this incident confirmed it. He was losing his mind.

Which, on the bright side, meant that I wasn't alone.

Several months later, we took Piper and Mabel to get spayed, and the vet called me to let me know they were non-compliant patients and I should probably come pick them up earlier than planned. I chalked up their nervousness to the fact that they'd each basically had a surprise hysterectomy, and wouldn't we all be a little out of sorts if someone surprised us that way? As it is, we have our whole lives to prepare for menopause, and a hysterectomy doesn't seem to make that process go any smoother from what I can gather.

Also, they had never been at the vet for an overnight stay other than that time Mabel decided to chase down a pack of wild javelinas, overestimating her size in an ill-advised pursuit.

It did begin to occur to me that we needed an option for boarding the sisters when we take vacations and such. So I spent a month or so doing some research to see what options might be available. Several people, including our vet, recommended a certain doggy day care/boarding facility, and I scheduled us for a trial visit.

We had an interview/orientation and I had HIGH hopes about how well the girls would act. A new dog park had opened in our neighborhood about two weeks prior, and I had been pleasantly surprised at how well they played and interacted with their fellow canines each time we visited, so I—FOOLISHLY—thought this would translate into their being awarded STAR CAMPER at the doggy camp.

Things went awry from the very beginning. Caroline and I had one heck of a time wrangling them out of the back of my car and into camp. Piper somehow wrapped her leash around my legs, and I fell. On the concrete. Fell. As in I skinned my knees, my hand, and an elbow. It was at this point that I began praying the camp counselors couldn't see what was proving to be a very inauspicious beginning to Piper and Mabel's camp experience.

We eventually got the girls through the door and into the check-in area. They verified all our paperwork, asked a few questions about their behavior, which I answered very optimistically, and then told us the girls were welcome to stay all day. They would take it from there. "No news is good news!" chirped the camp counselor as I limped toward the exit, nursing both my skinned knee and my pride. "But we'll call if there are any problems!"

Caroline and I drove back home, I poured myself a cup of coffee, and not even ten minutes later my phone rang. It was the camp counselor. "Um. Mrs. Shankle, Piper and Mabel are not really responding well to the camp environment. They are very stressed out, and we haven't even been able to work with them to the point of introducing them to their fellow campers."

"So should I come get them?" I asked. "Do we give it more time? I'm happy to do what you think is best."

"I think it's best if you come get them now," she replied firmly.

So that's how my girls got expelled from camp.

I made the drive back to the camp to pick them up, and I swear Mabel was smiling at me as she trotted into the check-out area. Mabel and Piper 1, camp counselor 0.

They didn't appear to be traumatized at all, although when I got them back home, they did exhibit some signs of shame. Piper kept giving me the side eye, and Mabel curled up in her bed and wouldn't even look at me. Of course, later I discovered she'd been busy writing some haikus in her journal.

Camp could not be worse
I have no need to make friends
Didn't even get s'mores
Billed as summer fun
Lying liars telling lies
Pack my bags, I'm out

But in a sign that this camp experience brought out her creative side, Mabel also changed the lyrics to the classic "Hello Muddah, Hello Faddah" and composed her own version.

Hello muddah, hello faddah
Here I am at Camp Bow Wowdah
Camp is very, very draining
And I would rather be in my own backyard even
        if it's raining
I went hiking with a terrier
Wished to bite him in the derriere
You remember I hate shepherds
There's one here that thinks he's faster than a
        spotted leopard
All the counselors smell like biscuits
And the kitchen has no triscuits
And the head coach has a shih tzu
So he thinks we should all just do what he do
Take me home, oh muddah, faddah
Take me home I hate Bow Wowdah
Don't leave me here with just my sister
I even miss Scout and he's not my favorite mister
Take me home, I promise I will not make noise

Or mess the house with all my toys
Oh please you hold the power
And I managed to get kicked out within an hour

While I appreciated her ability to write some catchy lyrics, it still didn't solve the problem of where the sisters could stay while we were on vacation. As it happened, we ended up boarding them at the vet. It wasn't my first choice, but when you're a canine delinquent, you find your options are limited. They were kicked out of two more doggy day camps (presumably for trying to sneak in cigarettes and sharing them with the other dogs while wearing black leather jackets), and then we briefly visited a fourth option, but I left before even attempting to board them there because the whole place felt too much like a maximum security prison. Ironically, that probably would have been the place that actually worked.

The good news is, we knew they were safe at the vet, and it was familiar to them. We thought about having someone stay at our house, but it takes the girls a long time to warm up to people they don't know, and they can be so wild that it's not a task for the weak. So basically, we need to make a strong, new friend who can come to our house on a regular basis and feed Piper and Mabel loads of treats. Or maybe just invest in a case of doggy Valium.

While we were at the beach, our sweet Scout passed away. Bruiser had died about a year earlier, but Scout was still hanging on, although he spent most of his time sleeping and passing what can only be described as the most horrendous gas known to man. And dog. He outlived two of his doggy companions, Jem and Bruiser, and he was a good grandpa to Piper and Mabel when they came along. He took them in stride and never minded that they jumped all over him and were constantly in his space. He was such a sweet boy, and I can cry now just thinking about him. He was my first baby. He loved us unconditionally in that way dogs do and never wanted anything in return other than the occasional belly rub. He was a good boy, and if it's true that all dogs go to heaven, then Scout will be one of the first in line.

I'd like to tell you Piper and Mabel came home from the vet after our beach trip and noticed Scout was no longer with us. A story about how they cried actual doggy tears and moped around for days. But that would be a lie. If they noticed he was gone, they showed no signs of grief. I knew Mabel wouldn't, but Piper seemed to enjoy having Grandpa around on the rare occasion when he wasn't sleeping, so I was surprised she never looked for him at all.

Mabel did write several haikus after our vacation and her stay at the vet:

> *All day in this place*
> *they want me to be their friend*
> *I bow to no one*
>
> *Dogs on my last nerve*
> *How long, O Lord, will I wait?*
> *Need my house, my bed*
>
> *Sister is so dumb*
> *Making friends to get more treats*
> *I will not be bribed*

And I guess Piper got bored enough to write a poem of her own:

I like food. Food is good. Please give me more of that food.
Where is my food? Food, food, food. I'd like more food.

These days, I take them to the dog park every day, which has become my saving grace for getting rid of some of their energy. As soon as they hit the gate, they take off running as fast as they can. Eventually, Piper slows down and just mills around and smells things like a normal dog. But Mabel never stops. She runs at full speed, constantly looking for a new dog to chase.

In fact, I looked at her the other day after we'd been there for a while, and her face was kind of sunken in from all the exertion and her tongue was hanging way out, but she was still frantically scanning the park to see if she was missing anything fun. I thought to myself, she's like the super-hyper kid on the playground you think is fun at first, but then want to avoid because she looks more than a little nuts and is scaring all the other children. That's when it dawned on me. Mabel is like the kid in the *Saturday Night Live* skit where Mike Myers plays a hypo-hyper kid who actually pulls a jungle gym out of the ground and runs down the street dragging it behind him after eating a Snickers bar and drinking a Coke. On the upside, if my car ever stalls at the dog park, I can give Mabel a Snickers bar and a can of Coke and have faith that she can tow me home.

I can't even imagine why Mabel and Piper got expelled from a place where normal dogs go and manage to act like they're not insane, but it does explain why they curl up in a ball around seven every night and barely move for twelve hours.

No amount of *My Dog Skip* prepared me for life with Piper and Mabel. Although it did show me how a dog can split your heart wide open in ways you never imagined. How can you love something so much when it simultaneously drives you crazy and prefers to eat your shoes instead of a fifty-dollar bag of gourmet dog food? How can you look at it one minute and wish it would quit barking and then the next minute rub its little head while using your schmoopiest Harlan Pepper voice to ask, "Who's the best dog ever?" and then answer for it, "I'm the best dog! I'm the best dog!"

It's one of life's great mysteries. And I wouldn't trade it for anything in the world. Not even a pair of flip-flops without teeth marks.

The Glamorous
Life of a Writer

Being a writer is 1 percent inspiration, 50 percent
perspiration, and 49 percent explaining you're not a
millionaire like J.K. Rowling.

Gabrielle Tozer

These days it seems like it's a rare weeknight when we all
sit down and eat dinner together as a family. Caroline
has soccer practice three nights a week because this is the new
American sports-obsessed way—apparently all of our children
are going to grow up to get athletic college scholarships and be
Olympic athletes. When you combine this with my schedule and
Perry's schedule, it all converges to create a lot of weeks where a
traditional family dinner is going to be the exception and not the
rule. On the upside, it has allowed me to drastically downscale
my dinner preparation game, and I basically end the week feeling
like Martha Stewart if I manage to cook just two meals, one of
which is always guaranteed to be tacos because Old El Paso just
makes it too easy with their Super Stuffer taco shells.

Anyway, it was during one of these family meals a few weeks ago that the conversation turned to famous people. Caroline told us that one of her friends at school discovered her family was distantly related to the Wright brothers. Or maybe it was Sir Isaac Newton. I can't remember that particular detail, and I'm not sure why my brain has decided it was either the Wright brothers or Isaac Newton. Maybe because one takes you up, and the other proves everything must come down. I'm probably not even right about either of those names and it's somebody like Amelia Earhart. I know there's some elaborate joke in here somewhere, but I'll spare us all by not trying to come up with it.

So Caroline was telling us about this friend being related to either the Wright brothers or Isaac Newton and finished it by saying, "I wish we were related to someone famous. Are we related to anyone famous?"

Perry pointed at me with his fork and said, "Mom." Caroline turned to me excitedly and asked, "Who are you related to that's famous?"

Here's the thing. I totally don't think I'm famous. At all. But I have written three books that all somehow ended up on the *New York Times* bestseller list, so some people might consider that an accomplishment. An accomplishment, by the way, that has clearly left my child less than impressed. In her mind, fame isn't something anyone has truly achieved until they're featured on Taylor Swift's Instagram with a #Squad.

I always tell people I never thought I'd actually get to write for a living, even though it was something I always loved to do. "Writer" just seemed like a fancy way of saying "I still live with my parents" or "I only wear sweatpants." (Based on how hard it has been for me to get a company to refinance our mortgage, this is a widely held belief.) So I did all the things you're supposed to do to become a self-sustaining adult: graduated from high school, went to college, got my degree, and then found a job I didn't really love just so I could pay the bills. Or at least most of the bills. I have always had a weakness for shopping, so I think there were several times in my first years out of college when I still needed my dad to bail me out every now and then. I have no doubt he was thrilled about this. Let's just say I was doing my personal, somewhat adequate best to be a grown-up.

It wasn't until after marriage, a child, and ten years of working in pharmaceutical sales that I started a blog on a whim late one night in July 2006. It was like my Hail Mary pass in the hopes of finding a creative outlet because I felt like that part of myself was dying. I had no idea what God was going to do with it or if I'd even stick with it for longer than a month, but over ten years later, that Hail Mary pass has proven to be more than I ever could have imagined.

For me, the dream of being a writer was born sometime in elementary school. I had a love of books that makes the phrase "voracious reader" seem not quite accurate enough. My first loves were books by Beatrix Potter, then Laura Ingalls Wilder, Beverly Cleary, and Judy Blume. These women all wrote words that meant something to me, and I got lost in their stories time and time again. I remember reading Erma Bombeck's syndicated column in the newspaper each morning and checking the Sunday paper to see what books were on the *New York Times* bestseller list. Somewhere inside of me was a little voice telling me that I could write a book someday.

Here's the thing: God puts dreams, both big and small, in our hearts for a reason. And it's no coincidence that our dreams most often line up with the gifts he has given us. Now, let me say that sometimes, as children, we can have other dreams that are just our imagination running wild, because I also had a dream of being Olivia Newton-John, but all those practice sessions of *Let's Get Physical* in the mirror while wearing a ballet leotard and leg warmers weren't ever going to make that dream a reality. And I'm eternally grateful for that.

What I'm talking about are those deep down, scared-to-even-voice-them-out-loud, heart-beating-out-of-your-chest dreams. The things that seem like they could be a reality if we can just get past our fear of failure and exposure and critics because all those elements are a real part of anything we are going to achieve in life.

J.K. Rowling was a single mom on welfare who dreamed that the name Harry Potter would one day be known by children everywhere yet had a manuscript rejected twelve times. Steven Spielberg was a kid with an idea about a large shark that terrorized a beach yet was turned down multiple times by the USC School of Cinematic Arts. Thomas Edison was told by teachers he was "too stupid to learn anything," and he invented the lightbulb, an invention with which you may be familiar. Walt Disney was fired for lacking imagination and informed that he had no good ideas. How stupid did that person feel later on, when a mouse in pants took over the world? The thing all of these one-time failures have in common is that none of them knew exactly how their leap of faith would turn out.

So many of us choose our path out of fear disguised as practicality: *I'll major in business; I'll get a sensible job; I'll keep dating this person because it's less risky than finding someone new.* I believe God wants us to walk out on the waters of our faith and calls us to things that are greater and deeper than any of our fears. And when we realize that failure at some point in life is inevitable—whether we're doing what we want or not—we might as well take a stab at doing something we love. We might as well go with the dream.

It makes me think of one of my favorite passages in *The Lion, the Witch and the Wardrobe*, when Mr. Beaver tells the Pevensie children about Aslan.

Lucy asks, "Is he—quite safe? I shall feel rather nervous about meeting a lion."

Mr. Beaver replies, "Safe? . . . Who said anything about safe? 'Course he isn't safe. But he's good. He's the King, I tell you."

When we open ourselves up to the life God has for us, it probably isn't going to look like what we had planned, and it isn't always going to feel safe, but it will be infinitely better because it's a life filled with purpose. And isn't that what everyone is searching for? Significance? A reason why we're here?

I transitioned from writing a blog to writing books almost by accident. I began blogging in July 2006 and spent the next two years writing for nothing but zero dollars and my love of telling stories. I didn't even necessarily have a huge "platform," as the marketing folks call it, but this was back in ye olden days of 2008, and the Internet was a different thing at that time because there was no Twitter, no Instagram, and not even much Facebook. Just blogs. #YeOldenDays. We barely even had iPhones. Just phones that flipped open and required you to text by pressing a number until it coincided with the letter of the alphabet you needed. It was essentially an updated version of hieroglyphics, and it's a wonder more of us aren't suffering from carpal tunnel syndrome. It also explains why I never texted anyone with anything other than a capital "A" which was my way of letting them know I'd received the text but wouldn't be responding to them with actual words or sentences unless I was on fire.

But it was in 2008 that I was asked to teach a workshop about blogging at the Proverbs 31 She Speaks Conference, even though all I could really add to the discussion is, "Hey, you can write things on the Internet, and people might read them." Lysa TerKeurst, the head of Proverbs 31, mentioned there would be agents and publishers there and encouraged me to put together a book proposal. So I went to Office Depot and bought a very professional plastic binder and then googled, "How Do You Write a Book Proposal?" It was all very sad.

While I was at the conference, I met with two publishers, both of whom told me no one would be interested in reading the memoir of a non-famous person. (I have refrained from sending them letters saying "I TOLD YOU SO!" because I am a bigger person than that. Well, not in my head but at least in actual actions.) But I did meet a great literary agent who saw potential in what I had put together, even though it more closely resembled a sixth grade book report than a book proposal, and called me six months later when I had given up all hope that I would actually ever write a book. The only problem was the publishing industry had kind of bottomed out with the rest of the economy, and no one was taking a chance on an unknown author at that time, so unless I changed my name to John Grisham or Danielle Steel, I essentially had no publishing options other than maybe going to Kinko's, paying them to print out what I had written, and putting it in one of their plastic binders. I also decided around that time that writing a book sounded really hard and wasn't something I wanted to do at all. Except for the little voice inside telling me otherwise. But then three things happened over the next two years:

1. The publishing industry rebounded.
2. Ann Voskamp showed the publishing world that a blogger could sell a lot of books, like half a million and counting. (This is very rare. It's like a unicorn sighting in the literary world, but it happened.)
3. I kept waking up every morning in a panic that there was something I was forgetting to do, and I knew in my heart that it was God not allowing me to let go of writing a book. It sounded a lot like, "Write that stupid book," because apparently God and I have similar personalities in my mind.

Ultimately, I threw caution, along with my pride and fear, to the wind and emailed the literary agent I'd had a few conversations with a few years earlier, and asked if he remembered me. He did. And he spent the next few months helping me figure out how to put together a book proposal for what became my first book, *Sparkly Green Earrings*. We received offers from several publishers, and like the most overused phrase ever from *The Bachelor*, my journey began. So whenever someone emails me and asks, "How do you write a book?" my answer usually is something along the lines of "You just have to write. And cry a lot. And hate most of what you write before you ever come up with something you can actually tolerate. And then read things written by other people that are so brilliant you want to die and never type another sentence. Also, sweatpants help."

For several months before my third book came out, people

kept asking if I was excited. And I was. Let me say that before I say anything else. Writing books had been a dream that was so deep inside me for so long that I don't know if I can even articulate what it means for it to come true. I still look at those book covers with my name on them, and it all seems like I'm playing an elaborate game of pretend.

I think being on the verge of having your third book release must feel a little bit like having your third child. You're not as naive. You know all the work that goes into it and that you're going to have some sleepless nights worrying about things beyond your control. You're trying to navigate that line between hoping people will buy your book and not being an annoying self-promoter. You know now that people can be mean and leave reviews that will hurt, even though you try to pretend you're totally cool with the fact that they just called your baby an ugly troll. Or maybe they just said you're a bad writer. Whatever. Same difference.

Maybe that's why I felt so overwhelmed. There were a few days when I thought to myself, "Well, I have officially begun my descent into full-blown agoraphobia," because I didn't really want to leave my house and I certainly didn't want to think about speaking events I'd already committed to or whether or not I'd commit to more. Because here's my little secret: I still feel so inadequate. Off the top of my head, I can think of at least 4,052 people who are better than I am. And that's on a good day.

That's what kept running through my mind. *I can't do this. I can't balance my time between work and family. I have no wisdom to share. I'm not enough. I'm not good enough, I'm not smart enough and, doggone it, I don't even know if people like me.* Stuart Smalley was a dirty liar.

Then one day I was driving to meet some friends for lunch and secretly wishing I'd get the flu so I would have an excuse to continue to be a social recluse (I'm envisioning you second-guessing your assumptions that we'd be friends in real life because now you're overcome with the realization that I'm so weird and introverted. Nothing makes me happier than when plans get cancelled.) when the song "Oceans" came on.

> *Spirit lead me where my trust is without borders*
> *Let me walk upon the waters*
> *Wherever You would call me*

As I listened—really listened—I felt God say to me, "You feel like this is too much because you're trying to figure out how to do it in your own power, and none of this is about you." It took everything in me not to just pull the car over and cry, because that's exactly it. I try so hard to be graceful and compassionate and kind and wise and discerning and loving, but I'm putting myself in charge of the production of all those attributes. And then my selfishness and pride and insecurity all rise to the top instead, and I freak out because I know how lacking I am in basically every category, and then I just want to sit on my couch in my pajamas and watch old episodes of *Friday Night Lights* because it feels safe.

Here's the thing. It's easier to sit on your couch than to risk failing. It's easier to sit on your couch than to be out in the world where you're vulnerable and open to being hurt or disappointed. But you know what happens while you sit on your couch in your pajamas playing Candy Crush and watching Tami Taylor? Real pants with buttons and zippers. Also, *life*. Beautiful, gorgeous, fragile, heartbreaking, mind-blowing life. God has a script written for each and every one of us, no matter who we are or what we've done or how ill-equipped for the adventure we feel.

We are all climbing our own versions of Mount Everest and have no idea if our oxygen will last or if an avalanche will come, but God does. We can never underestimate the grace and the strength he will give us for whatever he is calling us to do and whatever challenges we'll face. What he has planned for us is higher and deeper than anything we could ever hope to achieve on our own.

It's too much. It's too much for us to do in our own strength because we will mess it up, but he knows that and uses us anyway. It's never about creating or doing or being something that's perfect. It's not about having all the right answers. It's about being his. It's knowing that he who has called us is faithful.

I've always loved this verse: "He is before all things, and in him all things hold together" (Colossians 1:17). Notice how clear it is that we're *not* the ones who are supposed to hold everything together? God is holding it all. He is before it all. He uses the sinners and the weak and the ordinary things that this world views as broken and hopeless. But in him all those things come together and enable us to do things we never dreamed possible.

There was a time when I thought being a published writer would be a game-changer, that I would suddenly have an office that smelled of mahogany and own many leather-bound books. I will never forget the day my beloved editor texted me to let me know my book had made the *New York Times* bestseller list. I ran outside to tell Perry, and we hugged and I cried. We popped a bottle of champagne that night to celebrate. And you know what I did the next day? Scrubbed my own toilets and cleaned the tile in the shower. I tried to tell Perry that maybe I didn't have to go to the grocery store anymore since I was a *New York Times* bestselling author and he replied, "Um, I think you better get your *New York Times* rear end to the grocery store, because we're out of milk." Except he didn't say rear end. I did get to have my first television appearance on a local morning show, and Caroline encouraged me as only a preteen can, with "Bye, Mom! Please try to not act weird!"

Perfect.

The truth is, we can spend our lives waiting for the big thing to happen, the dream to come true, the thing that will change everything. And then it happens and it's nice, but guess what? No matter where we go, there we are.

The world tells us that true success is a certain amount in your bank account, a certain number of cars in your driveway, maybe that all kinds of people know your name and you write a book that inspires an entire theme park and a line of collectible figurines. But true success and prosperity comes when you are right where God wants you to be, doing what he has called you to do.

Or eating dinner as a family while your kid reminds you that in no universe are you famous. #NotSquad

To Exercise or Not to Exercise? That's Not a Real Question.

My favorite exercise is a cross between a lunge and
a crunch. I call it "lunch."

Author Unknown (but beloved and understood
in the deepest part of my soul)

In what is a true slice of irony, I'm sitting down to write this
chapter on the day of the Boston Marathon. A friend of mine
from high school is actually running it and has been document-
ing her experience on Facebook. Yesterday was carb-loading day.
I can totally get on board with that. Carb-loading day is what
I like to call "Wednesday." The part of a marathon that truly
troubles me is the running continuously for four hours part. Four
hours. And that's considered a pretty decent finish time. There
are some poor saps out there that will be running for closer to
six hours, or if they're like me, two days later as they try to finish
twenty-six miles.

The thing is, I absolutely believe in the importance of being physically fit. I've read all the magazine articles. I know it can lead to a longer life, better quality of life, and the ability to wear a swimsuit without wondering why a bunch of dumb-dumbs let swim bloomers quit being a thing back in the 1920s. But when it comes to exercise, I'm kind of like this guy, John, at church. Someone brought in a couple of dozen doughnuts and set them on the same table as the coffee urn to share with everyone, and John remarked to me later, "I went to go refill my coffee and accidentally ate two doughnuts before I remembered I'm supposed to be gluten-free." In that moment, I wanted to embrace him in a side-hug and whisper, "You, good sir, are my spirit animal." Because I would totally love to run a marathon someday and put one of those 26.2 bumper stickers on my car, except I keep forgetting that I don't like to run. Thus I don't ever want to run twenty-six miles at one time. Or over the course of two years.

Way back in 2008, two evil pandemics swept the country: the swine flu and Jillian Michaels' *30 Day Shred*. I don't know much about the swine flu, other than the fact that I believe pigs everywhere were being slandered for reasons that were beyond their control, and we are all going to turn into Howard Hughes if the media doesn't quit their fearmongering in an attempt to divert our attention from the real issues at hand, such as if there is really going to be a *Friday Night Lights* movie. I'm not talking about the one that already exists with Billy Bob Thornton. I'm talking about the one of my dreams starring Kyle Chandler and Connie Britton.

Here's a new topic for the media: Why won't Anthropologie send me even just one dish towel when I link to their site constantly? Is it some sort of fashionista prejudice because I am a forty-something mom and not their desired demographic? I believe the answer is yes, and that, my friends, is fashion profiling.

Anyway, unlike the swine flu, I did fall victim to the *30 Day Shred*. I can't remember when I first heard someone mention it, but I remember thinking they were kind of overly dramatic about the whole thing. And if there is one thing I cannot tolerate, other than reruns of *Golden Girls* and water chestnuts, it's someone being too dramatic. It makes me WANT TO PULL OUT ALL MY HAIR AND SET IT ON FIRE.

In fact, I vaguely recall thinking that I had mastered my *Fat Burning Pilates* DVD and had even reached a point where I could easily keep up with smug girl in the green sports bra (as I so affectionately referred to her), so what could the *30 Day Shred* possibly have to offer me? What new challenge could the *Shred* throw my way that could top *Fat Burning Pilates*?

I vividly remember a friend telling me she was on day eleven of the *Shred* when her teenage son walked in and mentioned that she had developed real, live ab muscles. I was impressed by this, because you know what teenage boys usually notice about their moms? Absolutely nothing. I personally hadn't seen my ab muscles since the second month of my pregnancy with Caroline. I figured the *30 Day Shred* might actually be worth looking into.

But then I just felt too tired to order the DVD from Amazon. Not to mention all the effort it would take to actually open up all the cellophane packaging and place it in my DVD player, because remember this was 2008. DVD players were still a thing, along with predictive texting, gluten, and Tom Cruise and Katie Holmes, better known as TomKat.

However, Jillian and I had a date with destiny, because as I innocently walked the aisles of Target one day, I happened upon the exercise equipment aisle, where I saw her staring me down, perhaps even daring me. I had no recourse but to buy the *30 Day Shred* and some lime green hand weights in the two-pound size because I am a risk-taker at heart.

I decided to wait until Monday to start my new workout regimen because I am a firm believer in procrastination, especially when it comes to anything regarding physical exertion. Why sweat today when you can sweat tomorrow? Also, it's always a good idea to plan to start something new on a Monday because even if the right Monday never actually comes along, you can keep believing that the following Monday holds the key to unlocking all your hidden potential.

But Monday came and I knew it was time to shred because I'd spent a whopping $15.99 on that DVD and couldn't let it go to waste. I believe I even told Gulley that I was starting it that morning as soon as we got off the phone and then laughed as I said, "It's ONLY TWENTY MINUTES! How hard can it be?"

I got off the phone and turned on the DVD. There was Jillian going on and on about how pain is fear leaving your body and blah, blah, blah, fast-forward to the real thing. She suggested that everyone start at Level 1. I decided I'd start at Level 1 to appease Jillian and her cut-off sweatpants, but figured I was really way past that since I'd been fairly consistent with my *Fat Burning Pilates* and elliptical workouts. And by fairly consistent, I mean I'd done them four or two times each.

Level 1 was an experiment in PURE HATE. I can't confirm this, but I am fairly certain it is something akin to what the CIA uses to get terrorists to talk. The static lunges with bicep curl combo was enough to get me to admit to anything I've ever done wrong in my life, including the time I stole a Brach's peppermint candy when I was four years old.

To add insult to total muscular injury, Caroline stood by as my alleged cheerleader, although she was actually more like a heckler in the audience at a comedy club. Do you know what's more aggravating than some muscular girl from a TV show taunting you with the fact that a four-hundred-and-fifty-pound person can do more jumping jacks than you? A five-year-old girl you gave birth to asking, "DO YOU FEEL THE BURNING, MAMA?" over a hundred times in three seconds. When I finished, I collapsed in a big heap on the couch, and in the words of Fred Sanford yelled out, "I'm comin' Elizabeth. This is the big one."

But I survived and felt compelled to do Day 2. In fact, I was determined to complete all thirty days of the *Shred* even if it left me completely incapable of standing upright or reaching for a bag of Cheetos. However, around Day 15 I began to pray I'd get the swine flu so I wouldn't have to work out with Jillian anymore. I figured if anything was going to kill me, my money was on Jillian Michaels and not some lame pig virus.

So I fell off the exercise wagon for a while. Or six months. But then I decided to try out this new sprint interval workout I saw on Pinterest. Mainly because it was a diet/exercise plan that featured a picture of Carrie Underwood's legs. And I don't know if you've ever seen her legs, but I would be happy to have a tenth of that muscle tone.

Who am I kidding? I'd be happy with less than a tenth.

Okay. I'd be happy with muscle tone. Period.

Anyway, this whole article on fitness said the key was not just to jog but to shock your body with sprint intervals and a lot of lunges and squats and other things that will make you want to cry. So I began a regimen of walking/jogging/sprinting through my neighborhood every morning, and when it was all said and done, I'm pretty sure my neighbors thought Phoebe Buffay had moved in. Because in my mind, I think I look as graceful as Beyoncé dancing when I run, but in reality it is much closer to a hippo stampede. And honestly, that's kind of an insult to hippos.

Apparently I'm not afraid of a little humiliation in the name of being physically fit, but you can imagine my disappointment when I looked in the mirror two days later and discovered my legs had yet to look like Carrie Underwood's, especially considering the last time I'd had that much of a cardio workout was running to get the dog off the carpet before he threw up. But I persevered and ate a small slice of ham for dinner with a side of steamed spinach. Then I texted Gulley and told her I felt like I was eating in prison, and that in no civilized setting is a hard-boiled egg considered an actual snack food. Not to mention that my body was going to need some time to adjust to all this fiber and protein and food people refer to as "fruits" and "vegetables."

That's all I'm going to say about that.

I also discovered that I think Greek yogurt is disgusting. The Greeks do many things well. Take, for example, the Olympics and the gyro, but yogurt is not one of them. I'm not sure all the reasons that it's supposed to be better for you than regular old Yoplait, but yuck. I bought a tub that was allegedly flavored like vanilla but tasted like thick cheese. While I like cheese in the form of chips and queso, I don't want anything vaguely cheese-flavored with that kind of density and texture mixed with berries and granola. I also don't want to eat like the cavemen ate because they would have totally eaten Hostess cupcakes if they'd had them, and last I checked, no one is pining for the days that you ate a meal consisting of wooly mammoth and some foliage that didn't even have the benefit of lemon pepper seasoning. As for eating gluten-free? I'll take all of the gluten that the rest of the world has given up. I'd like to open a bakery and name it Glutes and have an ad slogan that declares "All Gluten, All the Time."

Still, I pinned all these healthy eating sites on Pinterest because I decided I needed to learn to make more things that didn't contain cream of mushroom soup and cheese and pasta. I found some decent offerings, but some of the recipes were things like Roasted Beet Soup with Garlic. Yes, that is a diet food because no one would actually eat that. You'd roast those beets, puree them, pour them in a bowl, and then throw the whole thing in the trash when you realized it tasted like feet. No calories.

I just felt as though maybe my body needed a few weeks of shock and awe to remind itself that Oreos aren't a side dish, and six cookies after each meal might be considered excessive. Then I would plan to reintroduce a few of my favorite food groups back into my diet slowly, like chips and queso and guacamole and Gummies Sours Life Savers. Meanwhile, I'd continue to tear through the neighborhood with my arms flailing wildly to burn it all off and to have legs that looked like Carrie Underwood's. Oh, and to keep my heart healthy.

Because that's important too.

Although I have yet to see anyone putting up pictures of Carrie Underwood's heart on Pinterest.

Eventually, my search for the perfect exercise routine led me to something called Smart Barre. There is some variation of this in just about any city in America at this point, and the studios have various names that employ the word "Barre," always with an "E" on the end lest you not realize how superior you are if you do this variation of yoga/Pilates/ballet. A bunch of my friends had been raving about it, and there is nothing like peer pressure to make you try something new. This is how I discovered Bartles & Jaymes berry-flavored wine coolers in high school. But I'd also begun trying on sleeveless shirts in preparation for the upcoming summer months, and there is little that will serve to make you fully aware of your need for more exercise than carrying in a bunch of groceries and typing on the computer, which had essentially been my regimen for the last six months, than looking at your bare arms in the mirror. Be on the lookout for my new exercise video coming out soon entitled, *Here Are a Bunch of Groceries I Bought at HEB*.

Anyway, I wrongly assumed that since it was just a combination of ballet, yoga, and Pilates it certainly couldn't be that difficult. Isn't it just some stretching or something?

Yes. If they have stretching in hell.

I forgot that time I watched a documentary on PBS about ballerinas and the entire discussion of how much ballet requires of your body. You know how sometimes you work out, and you can feel your muscles start to shake in the middle of something? That was me. There was a point when I had to lift three-pound weights (I don't mean to brag about my impressive strength) until my triceps (I just googled "What are the muscles on the backs of your arms called?") were about to charley horse. I really thought I was about to shame my family name by dropping to my mat and writhing in pain and agony while singing out "Swing Low, Sweet Chariot."

If you've read anything I've written for, let's say, four or five minutes, you might know that I have a small tendency to exaggerate. But not this time. Even as I type this, the memory is causing my triceps to try to cramp up, and I had no idea typing even required the use of triceps.

But it wasn't just my arms. We worked our glutes and our quads and our abs. I thought a lot of bad words in my head when I had to semi-recline on a rubber ball and work some muscle in my stomach that I had never even been acquainted with prior to that point. Before I left that day, I signed up for the whole month because I knew it would make me feel like I'd have to keep my commitment—and I knew that otherwise I would never walk through those doors again. Partly because I wasn't sure my legs would ever work properly again. I was certainly aware that my triceps weren't going to help me propel myself off the couch. I couldn't even go to the grocery store because how was I supposed to carry all those bags with the things formerly known as my arms? At least that's what I told Perry that night when I informed him we were picking up Mexican food for dinner. After all, I'd burned all those calories at Smart Barre.

A few weeks later, as I drove to my 9:45 a.m. class, I finally pinpointed my real issue with working out.

You have to keep doing it to get and maintain results.

You know who I blame for this?

Jane Fonda.

That's right.

Some people are still angry about her stance on the Vietnam War, but that happened before I was born. All I know is that until she donned those black leg warmers for her workout VHS tape and then filmed *On Golden Pond* looking all tanned and toned and doing a backflip off a diving board in cutoff shorts and a bikini top, exercise wasn't really a thing. I mean, sure, some people did it, but it wasn't so much an aerobic workout or a social thing as much as it was maybe jogging around the block or standing on one of those jiggly machine things with a large band around you that was supposed to shake off your extra fat.

Now there's all this pressure to be "in shape" and "work on your cardio" and "quit eating ice cream for dinner." Pinterest is full of motivational quotes about working out like, "You don't get the bottom you want by sitting on it," and "Sore today, Strong tomorrow," and "Put Down the Doughnut, Loser." And then there's the whole CrossFit phenomenon in which people aren't content to just do their "Workout of the Day" or "WOD" as they call it, but also need to post videos of themselves doing it on Facebook. It's like Amway and Mary Kay had a love child who branched into the exercise business. You do you, CrossFit devotees, but with every video you post I'm only motivated to unfriend you instead of challenging myself to a series of workouts that seems likely to cause a serious knee injury.

All this pressure is why over the last several years, I've attempted everything from the *Couch to Almost, But Not Quite 5K* (that's my own personal version) to *Body by Bethenny.* There have even been a few days when I pulled out my Elle Macpherson workout video from college, although it's on VHS so it's safe that those days were circa 2002. I even went through a spell when I thought I could just work out at home and follow all the different workouts I pin on Pinterest. But then I discovered that pinning them doesn't count. You have to actually do them. Which is significantly harder to achieve.

All this to say that I'm really not sure why it just dawned on me, at forty-five years old, that exercise requires an actual lifestyle change, and sadly, is not like doing your income taxes, which only involves a few painful days and then it's all over for another year. You have to keep doing it on a regular basis, and if you quit for even a week, then you have to motivate yourself to start again. And eat carrots and whatnot.

So in the midst of all this self-actualization, here's what I have admitted to myself: I am not going to work out twelve months a year and eat healthy every day. Judge me if you want, but I'm just being honest about myself and my limited capacity to achieve long-term goals. I hate to waste my exercise energy on months like January and February when we can wear big sweaters and puffy coats and layers upon layers of clothing, plus I'm not caving in to the concept of New Year's resolutions because they only serve to give me an actual benchmark of how long it took me to fail. I believe January and February are prime Netflix months, and that's why God made them so cold. Plus, it's not like all those episodes of *Unbreakable Kimmy Schmidt* are going to watch themselves.

So I've recently adopted an exercise philosophy I like to call, "Oops, it's about to be hot, and I'll have to wear shorts" (trademark pending). The theory behind this is to wait until sometime around late March (this could even translate to mid-May for you northern girls) and then completely panic when the weekly forecast shows temps that will be in the mid-80s for the foreseeable future, and rush to sign up for the exercise class of your choosing.

As for my exercise of choice these days, I'm giving spin classes a whirl. Get it? Spin? A whirl?

This decision didn't so much come about as a result of my love for cycling so much as some friends of ours recently opened a new cycling place. My friend Debbi invited me to go with her for about two weeks until I finally ran out of excuses and went through the seven stages of summertime grief and said yes.

When I finally tried my first class, all I could think about was that old saying about how you never forget how to ride a bike. LIES. ALL LIES. Because even though it's a stationary bike, I felt a little bit like a cat who has accidentally found itself in a tap-dancing competition.

Debbi had promised me the whole thing was a no-pressure deal and I could ride at my own pace, but it turns out my own pace is "leisurely ride down the sidewalk," and we had an instructor who believed our pace should be "you are single-handedly responsible for pedaling hard enough to supply the entire city with electricity." At one point he walked to the back of the room where we were (Yes, I was in the back of the room. Hoping against hope to achieve invisibility.), and he got in our faces and yelled, "GO! GO! GO!" I'm not sure exactly what motivates me, but it is not that. Well, I take that back. It motivates me to kill someone with my bare hands but not to pedal a bike harder.

But I picked up speed and increased my resistance because I am just competitive enough to be a danger to myself, and long story short, I think I smelled popcorn burning before it was all over, which is one of the ten signs you're about to have a stroke. I read it on BuzzFeed.

However, when the class was over, I looked at my stats and realized I'd ridden almost fifteen miles and burned over five hundred calories. For those of you doing the wine math, that's two glasses. Not to mention I had tons of energy and felt super accomplished and basically had levels of excitement that most people reserve for accomplishments way more complicated than riding a stationary bike in an air-conditioned room while music plays and a disco ball lights everything up—you know, real accomplishments like running the Boston Marathon.

I'd like to believe that this time the exercise lifestyle will stick, and that I'm in it for the long haul. I'd like to say that exercise makes me feel levels of achievement I'll never feel after watching a Netflix marathon.

But I know none of that is true because history and Kimmy Schmidt have taught me otherwise.

Autocorrect Is the Devil

I know there's a proverb which that says "To err is human," but a human error is nothing to what a computer can do if it tries.

Agatha Christie, *Hallowe'en Party*

Listen. Once upon a time there was a thing known as a home telephone. It was a communication device people had in their homes, usually in the kitchen or another common area, and friends and acquaintances could call you and you would have conversations about boys or school or plans for the weekend. This usually led to stretching the coiled cord as far as it could possibly go in an attempt to reach your bedroom closet or the kitchen pantry in the hopes of having a semi-private conversation. Of course, this still didn't guarantee that another family member might not pick up the phone in another room causing you to have to sigh deeply and say, "I'M ON THE PHONE. HANG UP!" Because 1980s teenage struggles were real.

I spent a large portion of my high school years trying to convince my parents that I needed my own phone line. If only I had my own line and my own transparent neon phone, I could be just like Mallory Keaton on *Family Ties*. My kingdom full of scrunchies, Benetton apparel, and Final Net for a neon phone and a personal number.

If only I knew then that one day I would live in a world where we all have our own personal phones with our own unique numbers. With no cords. That allow you to talk to anyone at any time. And type messages back and forth while simultaneously watching videos of a cat wearing a shark costume and riding on a Roomba. Who are we, the Jetsons?

But here's what our past selves couldn't have warned our future selves about. All this technology, as wonderful as it may be, also has a tendency to make you look like an idiot at best and completely callous at worst. As if I don't have enough ways to make myself look stupid and sometimes incompetent, now I have my phone to help me, because there is nothing like the humiliation that comes when you text a friend who is going through a hard time in an attempt to say, "I'm so sorry," and the phone decides of its own free will to change your heartfelt sentiment to "I'm so sporty."

Sure. Because what I really wanted my friend to know during her time of grief and sorrow is that I have a lot of Lululemon leggings in my closet, and I occasionally wear them to do physical activity because I'm so sporty.

(I actually tend to wear them to go to the grocery store much more often than I use them for their intended purpose because the truth is, I'm not that sporty even if my phone says otherwise.)

I can't even talk about the time my best friend, Gulley, attempted to write a Facebook post on Thanksgiving Day to convey that she had "many things to be thankful for" and autocorrect decided what she really meant to say was that she had "many thongs to be thankful for." Yes, on this day commemorating that the Pilgrims and Indians shared food together in celebration of their new land, I want you all to know I am especially thankful for my skimpy underwear.

I remember when iPhones first introduced us to the concept of Siri. I couldn't wait to essentially have my very own personal assistant, so I drank the Apple Kool-Aid and immediately bought a new phone. As I was leaving the store, I asked Siri to text Perry on his cell to let him know I got my new phone. And she did it. I got a text from him a few minutes later that asked, "Is this you or Siri?" I told Siri to text "Siri." And she did it. Then he asked if the dishes in the dishwasher were clean or dirty and I told Siri to text that they were dirty. Except she texted "They're DARTY."

Oh, that Siri. Making fun of my accent and we've only known each other a few minutes. What a kidder! But that should've been my first clue.

When I picked Caroline up from school later that same day, she was thrilled to learn about Siri. I explained that you can ask Siri questions like "How is the weather?" and she'd answer. And so Caroline spent the next few hours SCREAMING things into my phone at poor Siri like "HOW DO MONKEYS WIPE THEIR BOTTOMS?" And Siri would say, "I don't understand."

Neither do I, Siri. Neither do I.

Siri did her best to answer Caroline. She'd pull up Google and search for "monkey's bottoms," but even Google has its limits. Then I read that Siri gets used to the sounds and intonations of her owner's voice over time and begins to understand requests better. And I lamented to Gulley that I was concerned Caroline had screwed up Siri forever with all that screaming and bizarre line of questioning because Siri and I seemed to have increasing difficulty communicating.

I'd ask questions that had been weighing on me such as, "Siri, why are the Kardashians famous?"

And she'd say, "I do not understand Kardashian."

"Me either, Siri. What's the deal?"

"I do not understand the deal."

Then came the day when I said, "Siri, call Gulley on her cell." She responded, "I do not see a Deli in your listings."

"NO, SIRI. CALL GULLEY CELL."

"Okay. Calling P.F. Chang's."

What the heck, Siri? What kind of mind game are you playing? So this is how it's going to be.

P.F. Chang's isn't even a deli. And I wasn't even trying to call a deli. I don't even really like sandwiches.

Then one of my friends on Facebook posted a cute exchange she had with her Siri. She told Siri, "Thank you," and Siri said, "No problem, Mary. It's my pleasure." This caused me to develop a complex that maybe the problems between Siri and me were because I neglected to tell her thank you. Maybe other people's Siris liked them better than mine liked me. Maybe Siri thought I was rude and ungrateful. And because I am neurotic, I actually conveyed this concern to Gulley, who replied, "There are enough problems in the world without people worrying about telling their phone, 'Thank you.' That's what's wrong with the world. People are worried about making their phone feel appreciated."

Yes.

People like her best friend.

I tried to thank Siri the next time she texted something to Perry for me, and she responded with "I don't know THANK YOU." Really, she was lucky I thanked her in the first place because her spelling was atrocious and she only understood half my words, and then I had to call Perry anyway to explain that we were having chili for dinner and not "jelly." I felt a little better when I read a story about someone who'd asked Siri to "Call me an ambulance," and she came back with, "From now on, I'll call you 'An Ambulance,' okay?"

Meanwhile, Gulley thought all of this was hilarious and loved to kid me about my concern that Caroline had been a bad influence on Siri and corrupted her from the very beginning, or that Siri's feelings were hurt because I didn't appreciate her. But that all changed on Christmas morning when Gulley opened up a brand new iPhone of her own. She set the whole thing up, synced all her information and then, eager to try out Siri for herself, said, "Siri, call my mom." Siri replied, "I don't know you and I don't know your mom."

Yes. Exactly my point.

Maybe she should have said, "Please."

A few weeks later, Gulley and I were at lunch with our friend, Donna. Her oldest daughter had just found out she'd gotten a really great summer internship. Donna laughed and told us that Avery had received a congratulatory text from Pop, her grandfather. But Pop sends all his text messages using Siri. So instead of sending his granddaughter a sweet, heartfelt message, Pop's text instead said something along the lines of "That's great about those mumbo jumbo hookers." Which isn't really a phrase you expect or want to hear from your grandfather.

Because Gulley and I have the sense of humor of two twelve-year-old boys, we decided it would be hilarious to just use Siri as our primary means of communication with each other over the next few days as an experiment in how wrong it could go.

I'll tell you what happened. Total and complete nonsense.

We sent each other things like, "I'm satisfied we can't go to lunch tomorrow at Alamo Café I was really happened we get data. I'll be satisfactory."

And, "You me and sister Garrett Allyn at half-right leaning Steve can't wait to talk to you."

For the record, I was not satisfied that we couldn't go to lunch at Alamo Café. I was sad. And I didn't really need any data. And hopefully it all worked out and I was satisfactory. I'm also sure that Sister Garret Allyn is a lovely person, and I can't wait to see her at half right-leaning Steve. Even though it's a shame Steve only leans half right. Was that a political statement by Siri? Who knows.

Finally, after several days of our fun at Siri's expense, we realized we needed to go back to normal texting. Mainly because we each had no idea what the other was trying to say. But Gulley texted me later and was concerned that one of her eyes was swollen and sent me a selfie so that I could see if she was imagining it.

(By the way, I'm absolutely sure this is exactly how Steve Jobs envisioned his technology being used. Well, this and being able to watch a hedgehog take a bath on your phone while you're in line at the grocery store. God rest his soul.)

So I looked at the picture and assured her the eye situation was her imagination. And then I decided to revert back to Siri, who took it upon herself to say, "You look beautiful. It's just that Bajando know how to capture Sarah Fossett."

I have always, ALWAYS, believed that Bajando know how to capture Sarah Fossett.

Now if I just knew exactly what that meant.

Other than the fact that Siri and I have a failure to communicate. And I don't think manners are really the problem.

The Leader of the Band

My life has been a poor attempt to imitate the man.
I'm just a living legacy to the leader of the band.

Dan Fogelberg

I just hung up the phone after a conversation with my dad. He
called, as he usually does these days, to recap Caroline's soccer
game the day before and to add his insights and thoughts about
her performance. I always say his boundless excitement regarding Caroline's athletic ability is the reason God didn't give him
an athletic child. His enthusiasm needed to be tempered with the
love and adoration that grandparents produce in spades. It's as
if that generational gap feeds the flames of what it truly means
to love someone with your entire being and believe that they are
capable of doing no wrong.

He likes to take credit for the fact that Caroline is so fast,
saying it came from all those times he chased her around the
yard as a toddler, causing her to squeal and laugh with pure
joy. And the truth is, while I don't think it was necessarily the
chasing that made her fast, her athletic skill does have a lot to do
with the DNA she gets directly from him. She looked just like

him the day she was born, causing Perry to declare, "She looks EXACTLY like your dad!" And while I don't know that it's a compliment to say your precious baby girl looks like an older Italian man, I loved that she looked like him, and I will say that as the years have gone by, she has kept the features that are to her benefit and lost the ones that might make her look like she could be part of the Mafia. She has my dad's long legs, his quick smile, and olive skin that causes her to turn golden brown as soon as the sun hits her. She'd also tell you, in a phrase she coined when she was little, that she and her Bops, as she calls him, share "a family resemblance for violence" because they both have a tendency to get irritated by all manner of small annoyances. I always say they are the true definition of a mutual admiration society.

Caroline has played soccer since she was in first grade, but this past year was the first year she was old enough to try out for the school track team. My dad talked about it endlessly and couldn't wait to see her run. Then she ended up getting sick for several days and was unable to try out for the team. I picked her up from school that day and asked if she was disappointed that she wasn't going to be able to run track this year. She assured me she was fine with it and maybe even a little relieved because we weren't sure how it was going to fit into our already busy schedule, but then she ended by saying, "I'm just worried about how Bops is going to take the news. He was so excited to see me run track, and you know, I'm his whole heart and soul."

I wanted to die at the sweetness. Because she couldn't be more right. She is his whole heart and soul. She has been since the moment he first laid eyes on her. He and Mimi drove all night from Houston after finding out I was in labor while they were at a Patsy Cline musical, and I don't know that he's ever loved anyone more. And what a gift to go through life with the certainty that you are someone's whole heart and soul. If she had been a boy, Perry and I would have named her Charles after him, but instead she turned out to be his beautiful little female mini-me, and I think he was more pleased about that than having a namesake.

The truth is, my dad has a way of making everyone around him feel like they're his heart and soul. He was the firstborn son of my grandparents, who were themselves the children of Italian immigrants. His family didn't have much, and he spent the first twelve years of his life living in what was essentially a one-room house. One of the stories he loves to tell about growing up was the time he was at his grandparent's house watching the chickens they let roam around the yard, when all of a sudden a huge rat came out of nowhere, grabbed one of those chickens, and dragged it down a hole in the yard. I realize this story doesn't mean his childhood was as rough as, say, growing up in a gang on the streets of Compton, but tell that to the chicken. What his family lacked in material possessions and chicken safety, though, they more than made up for in love. You have never met a group of people who would be as quick to take you in, feed you a meal, or hug you and kiss you right on the mouth before you leave. My dad carries their spirit of laughter, love, and the importance of family with him to this day, and it overflows to everyone he meets.

When my parents divorced in 1980, I didn't really know what it meant other than my dad wouldn't live in our house anymore. He rented an apartment less than a mile away, and my sister and I spent every Wednesday night and every other weekend at his house. He still attended all our school functions, and most importantly, called us on the phone every single night to see how our days had been and to tell us goodnight. I took all of it for granted. This was in the days before I knew that sometimes after a divorce, dads leave and start new lives and never call or visit. I didn't know he could have opted to just send a check every month and be done with it.

Instead, he eventually bought a house not too far away and took us shopping for twin beds and new bedding so we could decorate our second bedroom. He took us to Shipley's for donuts on Thursday mornings before he dropped us off at school and planned fun things for our weekends together, things like picnics and cookouts and taking us to Willowbrook Mall to shop. He stayed up late playing Donkey Kong with us on the ColecoVision he bought us for Christmas (You can have your Atari. Everyone knows ColecoVision was THE BEST and had amazing graphics that would make kids today be like, "Were these the video games cavemen played?") and watched *Smokey and the Bandit* with us for the four-hundred-and-fiftieth time. He was always open to letting us invite a friend over to spend the night, and I can't tell you how many times he must have cringed as he heard a bunch of little girls turning a game of Blind Man's Bluff into a full-scale pillow fight in the next room, but the beauty of a single, divorced dad's house is that he didn't have much in the way of breakable items. The only downside to our time at his house was that he never mastered the art of grocery shopping. All he kept in the way of snacks were raisins and nuts, both of which were beyond gross to us, so my sister and I often made our own snack out of dry spaghetti noodles dipped in peanut butter. How is that better than a raisin? I'm not sure.

Eventually, my mom moved my sister and me to Beaumont, which was about two hours away. Even then, he'd drive over to see us every other weekend or have my Me-Ma and Pa-Pa put us on a Greyhound bus to make the trek to Houston so he could have his time with us. (This was a simpler time, before the Internet, when people didn't know that maybe you shouldn't put your child on a Greyhound bus unless you wanted to end up as a cautionary tale on *Dateline*.) During those years, he still called every night to check on us. The truth is, I think I talked to my dad on the phone every night until I was married, and even now, we talk just about every single day. I think the upside to the divorce (if there's ever an upside) is that it forced us to forge our own relationship as father and daughter because we weren't able to rely on the mom to forge all the emotional connections.

When I was in college, I would often call him and ask him if I could take a road trip with some friends or something else that would require extra money and he'd always say, "Well, maybe I could sell a few of my suits." It became a huge joke with all of my friends, and we'd always refer to things by how many suits Charles Marino was going to have to sell to fund my latest adventure or mishap. For example, my wedding probably cost him his entire fall and spring wardrobe. He would send me a check enclosed in a note on his company letterhead, on which he'd written, "To keep you in the style to which you've grown accustomed. Love, Dad." Somehow he managed to walk the delicate parental line of giving me just enough but not too much along with setting expectations that were high yet attainable. And the truth is that while some people may struggle with seeing the graciousness and unconditional love of God as a heavenly father due to their earthly father, that aspect of faith has never been hard for me to grasp because of my dad. He never made me feel anything other than confident (perhaps a little overconfident) in my abilities while still showing me that anything worth having requires hard work and dedication.

After I met Perry and it was clear our relationship was heading toward marriage, Perry remarked that he felt like I still had some unresolved issues regarding my parents' divorce.

Really? Do you think so? But look how emotionally stable I am except for the times when I completely overreact to the smallest little feeling of abandonment!

Here's the thing: so much of what I had been told as a child wasn't that cut and dry in the bright light of adulthood, and the stability of marriage was at the top of that list. I asked my dad if he could come to town so we could talk about a few things that had been on my mind. We sat at Luby's Cafeteria just a couple of days later (which is really the best place to revisit any scars from your childhood because you can eat Jell-O afterward), and I asked him all the questions that had been piling up in my mind over the past fifteen years. He patiently and lovingly answered each one to the best of his ability, and while the details aren't something I feel I can share, I will say that while I had already spent my entire life up to that point being so proud to be Charles Marino's daughter, I never felt it more so than that day. He is a man of impeccable character and the utmost integrity, and he lived out what it means to take the high road even when the easiest thing in the moment might be to throw blame around. He put my sister and me before his need to be right, and now that I'm a parent myself, I can appreciate the fact that there isn't any act of love greater than sacrificing yourself to protect your child.

About a year later, my dad and I stood in the vestibule of Alamo Heights United Methodist Church, me in my wedding dress and he in his tuxedo. As the organist started to play

Pachelbel's *Canon in D* and my bridesmaids began to walk down the aisle, there were no words either of us trusted ourselves to say without releasing the floodgates of twenty-six years of love. He had loved me richly, protected me fiercely, and taught me everything that had brought me to that moment. I was leaving his care to walk toward the man who would take over where he was leaving off. Of all the good-byes I said as I left my wedding reception to begin my new life, the one I couldn't audibly say to him was the hardest. I just hugged him as hard as I could, whispered a teary thank-you, and ran toward the waiting car with Perry by my side. How do you thank someone for making you everything you are and showing you all that you hope to be? I think we both knew that even though that moment felt a little bit like the end of an era, it was also a whole new beginning. The thing about fathers and daughters is that little girls never forget their first hero, the first man who made them feel like they were the entire world wrapped up in a parade of Barbie dolls, dance recitals, freckled noses, bouncy ponytails, skinned knees, broken hearts, and high-pitched giggles.

My dad retired several years ago after spending almost forty years with the same company. They held a big retirement party for him to celebrate and invited all the people he'd worked with over the years, along with his family. I sat there that night and watched grown men get up with tears in their eyes and toast my dad, saying what he meant to them. I mean, he worked in the payroll industry; this wasn't a touchy-feely group of people. But he had given so many of them a chance to prove themselves, had mentored them, encouraged them, and made everyone laugh because he's never afraid to laugh at himself.

One of them told a story I'd never heard about a time my

dad shared with them that I had told my first-grade class my dad worked in "a jungle" because I'd heard him come home so many nights and say, "It's a jungle out there." And he was right. The world can be a jungle. There are always scary things waiting for you, the unknown lurking around the corner, things that go bump in the night; but what I saw that night was the way my dad had impacted his world and made it feel like a much better, safer place for everyone he encountered along the way.

One of my biggest regrets is that I didn't stand up and make a toast to my dad that night. I just couldn't. Some moments are so tender and take root so deeply inside you that you almost can't bear them, and that night was one of those times for me. It's one thing to know your dad is your hero, but to hear a room full of people echo the same sentiments will send you straight to the ugliest of all the crying.

But if I could go back, this is what I'd say. People talk so much about what it means to live an important life. What my dad taught me is that it's not about how much money you make, the car you drive, or any titles you achieve. He taught me by example that life is about showing up, living in the moment, and being true to who you are and what you believe, even when it's not the easiest path. Life is about your family, your friends, and your faith. It's about loving big, laughing hard, and enjoying a nice glass of wine. His love wrote the first chapters of my life and is the reason I never had to wonder if I was adored. He taught me what it means to be the same person at home that you are out in the world, and that you can never go wrong by making someone feel they are your whole heart and soul.

He is my hero, my leader of the band. The music of my life has been so much sweeter because of him.

Baby Sister

> There were once two sisters who were not afraid of
> the dark because the dark was full of the other's voice
> across the room.
>
> Jandy Nelson, *The Sky Is Everywhere*

My first real memory is of the day we brought my sister, Amy, home from the hospital. Actually, my first real memory is of the time I stubbed my toe while riding my tricycle, but that's the extent of that memory, and it only serves to explain my lifelong fear of sustaining toe injuries.

I barely recall my mom being pregnant since I wasn't even four years old at the time, but I do remember sitting on the emergency brake of my dad's beige Toyota Celica as my mom got in the car with my new baby sister. This was back in the days when people still believed kids should be allowed to roam freely in cars and that a center-console armrest was a perfect seat for a small child. You know, to allow them to see the road better. Or to get hurled out of the front windshield at top velocity. Either way.

I know I'm not the only child of the '70s who spent countless hours trying to sleep on the floorboards or in the back window of a Buick LeSabre. Obviously, God had a plan for my life, because between my daddy's road rage and the lack of any type of safety restraint, it is a wonder I did not have an untimely demise.

Amy was a colicky baby. She spit up a lot and had to be on a variety of special formulas due to some stomach issues. Thanks to modern medicine, we now realize that some of those intestinal issues could have been due to the vodka and Sprite my mom frequently drank throughout her pregnancy as part of her doctor's plan to ease her nausea. Of course, if you drink enough vodka, you eventually don't care if your stomach is calm or not. Considering the '70s were a simpler time, I guess we're just fortunate the doctor didn't suggest a good, old-fashioned bleeding complete with leeches and a pack of Marlboros to take the edge off. Good parenting in 1976 was essentially all about remembering to crack the car window so the smoke from your cigarette didn't suffocate the family while you blazed down the road listening to a Rita Coolidge eight-track tape. We've come a long way, baby.

Sisters can either be best friends or sworn enemies, depending on the day and sometimes the hour. It must be the combination of shared DNA and a shared bedroom that can cause you to love someone with everything in you one minute and be completely annoyed by the way they sound when they're breathing the next. There's a cassette recording my mom made on a little handheld recorder back when you had to push play and record at the same time. It captured me tormenting Amy at a young age. She's crying and whining as my mom is feeding her some of the few foods her stomach could tolerate while I sing-song in the background like only an annoying big sister can, "Amy! Amy! Look what Sissy's got! Rice! Potatoes! Ta-da! Ta-da! Ta-da!" and you can hear Amy begin to wail even louder as I lovingly point out that I have not one, but two starches for dinner that evening. Years later, we would listen to that recording and laugh while my mom merely wondered why she'd served both rice and potatoes for dinner one night.

When we were little, one of my favorite games to play with Amy was The Wizard of Oz. I loved to be Dorothy, and I could always count on my baby sister to be my faithful little Toto. She crawled after me everywhere I went anyway, so I figured I might as well make the best of it. I'd spread out my mom's old yellow comforter on the living room floor and travel down the yellow brick road as my little "Toto" crawled behind me and I commanded her to "bark louder!" Every now and then, I'd find a scrap of something on the floor that I'd feed her as a treat, because shag carpeting can reveal a lot of mystery items lost during previous TV tray meals eaten while sitting on the couch.

As we got a little older, I discovered the book *Freaky Friday* and thought it was the utmost in cleverness that the main character, Annabel Andrews, called her little brother "Ape Face." I quickly decided that imitation is the sincerest form of flattery, especially when it comes to insulting names for a younger sibling, and began to refer to Amy as Ape Face while encouraging all my elementary school friends to do the same.

I know. I was the worst.

However, in my defense, Amy did have quite the reputation on our street. She was known to make grown kids show up in tears at our front door to ask our mom if she would please make Amy give back their Big Wheels because she had commandeered it and wouldn't let it go without a fight. She was known to bite anyone and anything that didn't respond the way she wanted. I remember watching *Tom and Jerry* cartoons one afternoon when she snuck up behind me and bit me as hard as she could on my shoulder because she was so mad I was watching TV as opposed to playing whatever game she wanted to play. Everyone was a little bit scared of her in spite of how innocent she looked with her wrinkled-up pug nose, sweet smile, and Buster Brown haircut.

She got me back for making her play Toto and for the whole Ape Face thing the summer before I began fifth grade. My mom had gone back to work as a real estate agent, and my friends and I had some boys ride their bikes over to my house while the babysitter was there. This was strictly forbidden, but I didn't care because full-fledged boy craziness found me at a young age. (I blame this on both the movie *Grease* and all the Air Supply songs that were always on the radio.) Amy took blackmail to a whole new level and used this information against me for years. It cost me more nights of scratching her back until she went to sleep than I can count and many nights when I had to let her have the bigger cookie for dessert. Finally, around seventh grade, I decided the statute of limitations had surely worn out on this offense and told her to go ahead and tell on me. It was a relief like I had never known before, and my mom's non-response when Amy aired the story made me wish I'd come clean years earlier, because the entire sordid tale consisted of nothing more than a bunch of ten-year-old boys loitering out in front of our house on their bicycles while we giggled at everything they said.

One of our fights is so legendary that to this day, we refer to it as:

The Black Sock Debacle of 1988

It was the fall of my senior year of high school, and I was truly a pleasure to be around. Like most seventeen-year-olds, I had the world completely figured out and certainly didn't need anyone telling me how to live my life, much less breathing air in my presence. I was so cool in my own mind that I sincerely believed the only reason Simon Le Bon from Duran Duran wasn't dating me was because he hadn't met me yet. Amy was in eighth grade and attended a private Christian school which required her to wear a uniform every day, except on the one day a month deemed "Free Dress Day."

Since I attended public school, my wardrobe was significantly larger than Amy's, not to mention full of sophisticated items like Reebok high-tops, a Guess miniskirt, and Girbaud jeans, along with a lot of shirts with shoulder pads and various bedazzled treatments. This resulted in Amy usually borrowing something of mine to wear on Free Dress Day because if you only have one day a month to express your style, you want to make it count. Anyway, on this particular Free Dress Day, she wanted to borrow my black socks.

Now, we could spend a few hours discussing why I even had black socks, much less socks in every color of the rainbow, but that's beside the point. And honestly, I have no explanation other than to say that the late '80s were an unfortunate time in fashion, and all the misfortune included therein can basically be summed up with the words "acid-washed."

I told her no. The black socks were off-limits.

What was I? Some sort of teenaged Anna Wintour? The devil wears black socks? Why on earth was I so stingy with my black socks? It confirms my suspicions that I may have not been living as my best self in 1988. Lo and behold, Amy believed strongly enough that her outfit couldn't be all it was intended to be without the black socks so had the audacity to sneak into my room, take them, and wear them in spite of my denial. I was infuriated. I was enraged. I threw a fit about the thievery of my black socks and perhaps even went so far as to launch into a tirade about a lack of moral character, which was really gutsy and hypocritical, considering I'd spent the weekend before hosting a secret "get-together" for some friends while my mom was out of town that involved one of them drinking until she threw up in my sister's bed. And while I am sure my mom thought this whole black sock situation was one of the dumbest incidents she had ever dealt with, she was forced to punish my sister for taking something that didn't belong to her, even if that something was a cheap pair of black socks.

Amy got grounded for wearing my black socks.

And I was glad.

I would like to publicly acknowledge right now that perhaps I pushed the sock incident too far. Maybe I should have been a little more forgiving and understanding about how a thirteen-year-old girl, forced to wear a hunter green plaid skirt and matching vest on a daily basis, could have been driven to steal a pair of black socks, because when you think about the unspoken freedoms a pair of black socks can convey, it's totally understandable.

That was our relationship in those younger years. Amy was the baby sister always sizing me up, competing in everything, including brushing her teeth faster, making better grades, and making better decisions. Once I got my driver's license, there were days I had to pick her up from school. I'd pull up with the sunroof open and the music blaring, then drive way too fast on the way home while she yelled at me to "SLOW DOWN OR I'M GOING TO TELL MOM!" She was the good one, the studious one, the responsible one. Maybe that's why I got so much satisfaction out of getting her in trouble for taking my socks.

Having a sister can be one of those things in life you take for granted. After all, it happens with basically no say-so from you, and it's a built-in relationship that is as much a part of you as an arm or leg. You don't get to choose whether you want it; it's just part of who you are. There were times when the almost four years between us seemed immense, and times when that age difference didn't matter at all. We have each alternately thought the other was dumb, bossy, wonderful, maddening, amazing, someone we couldn't live without, and a total pain in the rear end.

When we were little girls, there were days we would get totally immersed in our relationship and play Barbies forever, have dance parties, build forts, and curl up in bed together at night whispering secrets and dreams and fears. There were times when our childhood looked scary, and we were there to reassure each other that it was all going to be okay. And then there were times when we'd get so mad, we'd shut each other out with silence and slammed doors. But at the heart of it all, Amy is the only person in the world who shares my entire life story. Our relationship has a shorthand unique to sisters because we each know what the other means even when it's a one-word exchange. In so many ways, we survived not just with each other, but because of each other.

Little did I know that the same annoying sister who ill-advisedly took my black socks would be the same person who would help me keep my sanity after Caroline was born. At that point, Amy didn't have children of her own yet and was more than happy to come over on a daily basis and hold Caroline for hours while I did such novel things as shower, cry, and brush my hair. She'd sit on the couch with me and hold Caroline while I sat in my purple, spit-up-stained chenille robe and cried (a combination of sleeplessness, feeling overwhelmed, and a potent cocktail of postpartum hormones). I am forever grateful for the afternoons she spent on my couch when she could have been doing so many things that were more fun than watching your big sister have a meltdown, like going to the dentist. Watching her hold my baby girl and seeing how much she loved her, just because she was mine, made me realize even more that there is no gift like a sister.

Sometimes you're fortunate enough to have one of your best friends born right into your family. You know each other's stories, you feel each other's pain, you rock each other's babies, and you hold each other's hands as you go through life. You forgive the bad, remember the good, and are forever grateful that there is someone in the world who knows you so well and loves you anyway. Even when you used to refer to her as Ape Face.

Dodging a Bullet

It was a million to one shot, Doc. Million to one.

Frank Costanza, *Seinfeld*

S ome of you may remember several years ago when then-Governor of Texas Rick Perry shot and killed a coyote during his morning run. It made national news because the rest of the United States was all like, "What madness is this?" while most people in Texas were like, "We call it a Tuesday."

I identified with the story because we have had an infiltration of coyotes in our neighborhood over the years. We live right on the edge of a wooded basin that tends to flood at least once every few years, causing all the wildlife that normally live there to head for higher ground. Unfortunately, this higher ground is also called "my backyard." There was a time about ten years ago when we trapped over twenty-seven raccoons, sixteen possums, and seven skunks, otherwise known as trash cats, night rats, and stink squirrels, in our backyard over a six-month period. It's like we inadvertently put up a billboard advertising our backyard as the hot new wildlife club in town. Thursday night is Lady Opossum Night, and trash is free until 10 p.m.!

With this infiltration of rabble-rousers, who skitter and skritch and search through your trash like they're trying to steal your identity, came the coyotes. There used to be a couple of chickens who lived at the end of our block, and every now and then, we would drive by in time to see one of them crossing the road, causing Perry or me to predictably ask, "Why did the chicken cross the road?" because we are never ones to pass up that kind of golden opportunity. But after the coyotes made themselves at home in the neighborhood, the chickens were suddenly never seen again. I think we all know what happened. The chickens opted to move to a nice, big farm in the country where they could roam free and raise their babies without the worries that come with big-city life, such as chicken gang violence and rooster drug dealers. I will not discuss the alternative scenario.

However, it wasn't just the chickens. All of a sudden there were signs everywhere that read, "Have you seen this cat?" or "Help! My Chihuahua is missing!" and I hate to be heartless, but we've all seen *The Lion King* and know that the animal kingdom can be cold and cruel, no matter how many animal videos you've watched on YouTube that try to prove otherwise. For every elephant that cuddles up with a puppy, there's a hippo that will tip a canoe and chomp some villagers with his giant teeth that look like marshmallows but are decidedly not made of sugar.

One morning when Caroline was still small enough to be pushed in a jogging stroller, Perry and I were taking a walk with her and our dogs when we spied a coyote staring at us from about thirty yards away. He was particularly intent on Caroline; she must have looked like a bite-size treat with a bonus cup of Cheerios thrown in. Perry used his cell phone to call our neighborhood police department and report the coyote sighting as we hurriedly put distance between ourselves and Wile E. We stopped to watch as a police officer showed up on the scene and pulled a .22 rifle out of the trunk of his car, aimed at the coyote, and proceeded to miss him three times before the coyote finally turned and made his way back through the woods whence he came. I guess if you want a coyote shot properly, then you better hope the governor is around and not just the local police force.

Anyway, I tell you all of this to make the point that sometimes things are a little different in Texas than they are in the rest of the United States, and lo, the world. We are a state that was founded by outlaws and immigrants in search of land and adventure, and much of that spirit still remains. It should really come as no surprise that there is an actual training program in Texas whereby you can become certified to shoot wild hogs from a helicopter. This is officially called "Aerial Wildlife Management." I realize if you live in New York or somewhere of that nature, this may sound absurd, but wild hogs are an actual problem in Texas and tend to destroy everything in their path. Not to mention that they reproduce at a rate that would make rabbits and the Duggars jealous. It is a constant battle to keep their numbers in check.

Perry participated in several helicopter hog hunts as an observer but decided a couple of years ago that he would like to become certified to shoot them himself. Maybe you're already doing the math in your head and realize this requires both shooting a gun and flying in a helicopter. What could possibly go wrong?

The morning of the certification process, he drove to the appointed testing location. I didn't hear from him for several hours. I had no idea how long it takes to prove you can bring home the bacon from a helicopter, so I wasn't necessarily concerned until he called me and said, "Hey, I'm on my way home now, and everything is okay, but there was a little bit of an incident."

"What kind of an incident?" I asked.

"I kind of shot myself in the head," he replied.

Well. This is very normal. Let me tell you a story about a wife who hears that her husband has shot himself in the head and begins to freak out. It's called RIGHT NOW.

He assured me he was fine, then said, "I'll tell you the whole story when I get home, but I just want to concentrate on driving because I have a little bit of a headache."

I would think so.

When he walked through the back door an hour later, I wasn't prepared for the enormous bandage on his forehead, not to mention the dried blood covering his face, his neck, and the front of his shirt. Hey, next time maybe bring a change of clothes in case you accidentally shoot yourself. Fortunately he seemed to be okay, and the actual wound was much smaller than I originally thought based on the enormous gauze bandage and all the blood. It seems your head bleeds profusely at the least little thing.

Perry explained that they were up in the helicopter, and he was firing shots at the various targets when one of the bullets ricocheted off the metal and grazed his forehead. He was most proud of the fact that he never quit firing, in spite of the blood running down his face and clothes.

He said, "The instructors couldn't believe it happened. They've never heard of it happening to anyone, ever. We all agreed it was a one-in-a-million shot!" Then, he added with a flourish, "Best of all, I found out that I not only qualified as a licensed shooter but received an EXPERT rating, which less than 5 percent of all people achieve!"

Yes, that is the best of all. That and the fact that you are still ALIVE.

You know what you never think about when you meet the person you want to spend the rest of your life with and you're coming up with clever hashtags like #MelAndPerryGetMarried or #PerryAndMelWeddingBells or #GoingToTheChapelAnd-GoingToGetPerry'd? (I know. Perry'd. I'm inordinately pleased with myself right now.) You don't think that one day maybe your beloved is going to accidentally shoot himself in the head while flying in a helicopter and then believe the most noteworthy thing from the day is that he qualified as an expert shooter. You have hopes and dreams and plans, but not one of them includes that scenario. In fact, there are many things that are going to happen over the course of a life together which you can never anticipate, no matter how many cute engagement pictures you take while holding a chalkboard with "I DO" lettered artfully across it.

I used to love buying copies of *Brides* magazine way before I was even anywhere close to becoming a bride. Maybe part of it was growing up in a home where my parents were divorced, or maybe it was all the times I watched *Cinderella* or—even more so—Danny and Sandy from *Grease* ride off into their happily ever after, but marriage was what I wanted more than anything. The problem is, we can get so focused on the big moment—the proposal, the wedding, the honeymoon in the Bahamas—that we have no idea about the reality of what happens next.

And what is that, you ask? Well. It gets complicated. There are births and deaths, love and loss, tears and fighting, laughter and joy. There are bank accounts that never seem full, kids who interrupt you constantly, car pools to drive, groceries to buy, and dinner to cook. It's a constant push and pull of what you want versus what he wants, and ultimately, the compromises you're willing to make. It's never knowing you could love someone so much one minute and then be yelling at them the next minute for something as dumb as not throwing away their Band-Aid wrappers.

It's realizing that the things that define a successful marriage have nothing to do with the wedding dress you choose or whether you decide on the Italian cream wedding cake or opt for plain white icing or find the perfect song for your first dance. It's not the big moments that make a marriage work but all the little things that remind the other person how much they matter. Reaching for a hand, saving the last cookie, driving soccer car pool, stopping at the grocery store for milk, letting it go when the other person says something stupid, and taking the time to look each other in the eyes. Little things that help you remember that before all this chaos you've created together, there were two people in love. And that the whole thing can be so fragile because you never know where life is going to take you next, especially when one of you likes to shoot hogs out of helicopters.

And that maybe this life you've made together is the ultimate one-in-a-million shot.

Small Things

Things That Keep Me Up at Night

"I'm tired of overthinking every single thing, you know?"

Tim Riggins, *Friday Night Lights*

Almost every weekday, I pick up Caroline from school. This requires sitting in a line of cars for anywhere between ten and twenty minutes, depending on how early I arrive and how long it takes my girl to pack up all her stuff and make her way out to my car. On most days I use this time to do very important things like check Twitter or Instagram, send funny Snapchat photos to Gulley, or return all the texts I've neglected to send earlier in the day. But sometimes I just listen to the radio, and that's what I was doing the other day when all of a sudden, an ad came on with a deep, authoritative male voice that asked, "Does your teenager have yellow toenails? Have you noticed that your teenager's toenails seem thicker than normal?"

My first thought was "EEW." I love my child, but I do not really want to think about her feet. My second thought immediately followed, and it was a level-ten reaction along the lines of, "WHAT DOES IT MEAN IF MY TEENAGER HAS YELLOW TOENAILS? IS IT A SIGN THEY'RE USING DRUGS? DOES IT MEAN THEY HAVE AN EATING DISORDER? IS IT A WARNING THAT THEY HAVE A HEART CONDITION?" As it turns out, yellow toenails in your teen are nothing except a sign they might have a toenail fungus. Which means my initial response of "EEW" was the appropriate one.

This is the hell our Facebook culture hath wrought. Everything is something to worry about. I never knew a child could drown hours after leaving the pool, but I know it now, thanks to a Facebook article. I didn't know you could be electrocuted jumping into the water off a boat dock, but I know it now. I didn't know there is an amoeba that lives in certain lakes, and if you swallow it, you could die. Or that if you see a pair of shoes hanging on an electrical line near your home, it means someone is selling drugs nearby. Thanks, social media, for taking fear and anxiety to an entirely new stratosphere. You are the best. One quick question: where can we send the bill for the medication we have to take every night in the hopes of turning off our brains long enough to get some sleep without worrying about all the ways we and our loved ones could possibly die?

Here are the things that keep me awake or can ruin a perfectly good day when my mind goes to the dark place. (Disclaimer: This is by no means a comprehensive list but rather a random sampling. Because one of my fears is that if I were to show you all my crazy, then you might put this book down and never pick it up again.)

1. Did I remember to blow out the candles I lit earlier to get rid of the fried fish smell in the house?
2. What's that noise? Is there something outside my window? Is it a raccoon, or worse, a clown?
3. Did I overpluck my eyebrows again?
4. How do I balance keeping Caroline off the worst of social media but still let her engage with her friends?
5. What if something happens to Perry on a hunting trip?
6. Is that a lump I feel? What if I have cancer? What if Perry gets cancer? What if Caroline gets cancer?
7. Did Caroline finish her homework? Should I remind her to finish her homework, or should I let her deal with the consequences?
8. What am I going to cook for dinner and/or pack for school lunch tomorrow?
9. Should I keep those new shoes I ordered? Do I really like them or just kind of like them?
10. What am I going to do when Caroline leaves for college in five years?
11. What if everything Fox News tells us might happen really happens?

12. Will we be able to afford college and still retire before we're eighty-five?

13. What if an alligator rings my doorbell? (This actually happened to someone. I saw it on CNN.)

14. Should I turn off my phone? Are the wireless signals from our phones going to give us all cancer?

15. What if I turn off my phone and there's an emergency?

16. Did I remember to set the DVR to record *The Bachelor*?

17. Will Piper and Mabel suffer from depression when we have to board them while we're on vacation?

18. Should I quit eating gluten? Should I try the Whole30 diet? Do I need to exercise more? Are we out of Sour Patch Kids?

19. Do I need to clean my oven? Is it true that the self-clean feature can cause your oven to break, or worse, burn your whole house down?

20. Am I supposed to be this worried about things? Am I worrying too much? Should I worry more? Are there things I should be afraid of that I don't even know about?

I once heard someone say that the best way to combat your greatest fears is to speak them out loud. It causes them to lose a little bit of their power. And if that's the case, let's hope this does the trick so that I didn't reveal the deepest and sometimes dumbest parts of myself in vain.

When Life Is a Mixture of Sweet and Sad

Where you used to be, there is a hole in the world,
which I find myself constantly walking around in the
daytime, and falling in at night. I miss you like
hell.

Edna St. Vincent Millay

I have known since junior high that there is really no angst
like junior high angst. Those years are rife with unfortunate
haircuts, hormonal acne, and questionable fashion choices. That
those things also coincide with an awakening that maybe boys
aren't such a bad thing after all is a recipe for a lot of feelings.
And by a lot of feelings I mean a junior high girl can completely
suck all the emotional oxygen right out of any room.

A friend of mine, who shall remain anonymous to protect
the innocent, told me years ago about her then-junior-high-aged
daughter and how she made graphics to post on Instagram that
said things like, "I'm in love with a person I've never met and

193

a city I've never been to," or a list of her favorites that included "listening to old record albums while burning candles in my room." My friend told me, "We don't even own a record player, and she's not allowed to burn candles in her room!" But junior high girls aren't ones to deal in reality when the drama they can create is infinitely more satisfactory and tumultuous.

At the time, Caroline was still in elementary school, so I hadn't experienced any of this from a mother's perspective, but we have now arrived at that juncture. Thus, I was thrilled when her seventh grade English teacher invited us to the class poetry reading. Sure enough, there were poems written by the girls about things like transparency, heartbreak, and wearing a mask, while the boys stuck to familiar ground such as fishing and football. But I cannot judge, seeing as I am the one who once wrote these words in my own junior high poetry book entitled *Except for One*:

> *All my friends were sympathetic*
> *Except for one*
> *Because she was his someone else*

That particular piece was penned late one night after a dance at the local YMCA where I'd had immediate regrets about breaking up with my eighth-grade boyfriend hours earlier. So much drama, so little sense.

Fortunately, Caroline is much more level-headed than her mother has ever been, and so her poetry is actually about real things as opposed to manufactured romantic intrigue. She had to write a book of five poems for her seventh-grade English final, and as I was reading through her words, I was struck by one line in particular: "some people stand out more than others, like neon posters on a beige wall."

I wondered if she sees herself as the beige wall or the neon poster, because she is nothing if not a neon poster kind of girl. But the junior high years can cause you to question everything from the way you look to what you believe as you and your friends grow and change at such a rapid pace.

The following weekend, I was at the pool with Caroline and one of her best friends, Maddy. As I watched the two of them jump off the edge of the pool and laugh until they cried and talk endlessly as they baked in the sun, it dawned on me that this kind of friendship is what helps you be a neon poster. It's the knowledge that you have people who know you and love you and encourage you, who help you be the best and brightest version of yourself. So I thought it was fitting that Caroline ended her poem with a line about how sometimes you may not notice the beige wall, but it is the thing that holds up the neon poster. The beige wall allows the neon poster to shine bright.

One of the reasons I'm so fascinated by having a daughter who falls closer to the neon poster end of the spectrum is because I spent years seeing myself as more of a beige wall. It's true. I wanted to be the girl who dances without feeling self-conscious or tells the funny stories that make everyone laugh and believe the party wouldn't be half as much fun without you. But as I've gotten older, I've realized the truth is that we should all have a little bit of neon poster and a little bit of beige wall in ourselves.

Sometimes our role is to be brighter than the sun, and sometimes our role is to sit back and cheer on our friends as their gifts are on display. My friend Jamie's mom once told her, "Every relationship has a peacock and a grouse." I think that's true.

When I look at my closest friends, I can totally see a pattern. I am drawn to peacocks. I love being surrounded by funny, witty, bright, strong-willed women who aren't afraid to take charge of almost any situation. I tend to approach social situations—and life—a little more cautiously, and the friends I have chosen along the way have taught me the joy of jumping in with both feet, embracing a challenge, and not being afraid to love with your whole heart. We all love each other fiercely. They are my cheerleaders, my first call, my sanity, and a big chunk of my heart.

This is why it was so devastating when, five years ago, one of us found a lump in her breast. Jen is one of my closest friends and was my college roommate. She is also one of the funniest and warmest people you could ever hope to meet, a neon poster if there ever was one. She was just shy of her fortieth birthday and still nursing her seven-month-old son when she realized she had a lump that wasn't going away, which made her decide it might be more than a clogged milk duct. Sure enough, a biopsy confirmed her fears, and it started us all on a journey that none of us ever wanted to take. That first round of cancer involved chemotherapy, a lumpectomy, and radiation. It was a hard road for Jen and a hard one for us to watch her travel, especially as she balanced being a wife and mom on top of all of it. But she made it through and got the all-clear from her doctors almost a year from the day she was first diagnosed. We all breathed a deep sigh of relief and said prayers of gratitude that we had gotten our miracle.

When I was writing my book *Nobody's Cuter than You* (It's all about friendship, in case you haven't read it, and is available at bookstores everywhere. Pardon the shameless promotion, but I just thought two of you might be interested.), Jen was about six months into her new, cancer-free status, but as I wrote the book,

I texted her to clarify a few details about her diagnosis, because I wanted to make sure I was getting the timeline right. It was in the midst of a flurry of text messages back and forth that Jen texted, "Truthfully, I don't believe it's the end of my cancer story. But I can be thankful for now that there's 'no evidence of disease,' as they say. And I'm not scared of the future either, which is such a gift!"

When I read that text from her, I got chills down my spine because the cancer felt like Lord Voldemort and was He Who Must Not Be Named. Plus, I had naively assumed that the all-clear meant all-clear forever, and we had fought that battle and come out on the other side. But Jen sent that text on October 2, 2014, and on December 6, 2014, we found out that her cancer was back with a vengeance.

Gulley and I always reserve the first weekend of December for our Christmas shopping weekend. We start on Friday morning and use the entire weekend to finish all our Christmas shopping and even get all our presents wrapped. The fact that we find time in between all of this to drink wine and go out to dinner and sleep in late is just a bonus. So we were out shopping on Saturday, December 6.

We'd made our way out of the house late that morning and hit a few stores on our list. We were beyond pleased with our progress, because we were breaking all manner of Christmas shopping weekend records. We even made it to The Container Store to pick up wrapping paper while it was still light outside. This turned out to be fortunate because it allowed Gulley to fully appreciate a man parked next to us who was wearing a red T-shirt with a white Santa beard down the front while drinking a can of Budweiser through a straw. He rolled down his window and said to Gulley, "I'm gonna tell you like I told that woman in there, you ever seen me and Santa in a room together?"

Well. No.

No we haven't. Also, I don't believe we asked.

We pondered our thoughts on this man as we made our way to our neighborhood Target. It was, by the way, our third Target visit of the weekend but served to confirm that our Target is the best of all the area Targets. While we were there, we both heard our phones ding with an incoming text and checked them, only to discover our friend Jamie was texting us to let us know that she had been at the hospital all day with Jen, and that the doctors had said Jen's cancer was back. Which is how Gulley and I found ourselves crying in the gift wrap aisle at Target at 5:38 p.m. on a Saturday evening.

I spent those weeks before Christmas in a little bit of a haze. The holidays are always so busy anyway, and Jen's cancer was like a bruise you forget about for a minute until you bump it again and remember it still hurts. One night, a few days after that initial text from Jamie, I was in the middle of helping Caroline finish a science project (this is squarely not in my set of skills or life goals) when I received a text update from Jen to several close friends that basically let us know her hard news had just gotten harder because a follow-up appointment to the doctor discovered the cancer had spread to her lower back, ribs, lungs, and more lymph nodes as well as more spots on her liver than they had originally thought.

Honestly, as I read her text, I didn't even let myself process it because I knew I couldn't without falling apart. I still had to help Caroline finish making videos showing the difference between physical and chemical changes, cook dinner, and get everyone settled in for the night. So I felt tears in my eyes and then quickly compartmentalized it into "Things to Think about Tomorrow," which I learned from Scarlett O'Hara.

The following day, I woke up and discovered Jen had posted the news on her blog along with an update that she was headed to Houston to see some specialists there on Friday. Since my parents, Mimi and Bops, have a house in Houston, I texted her and asked if she had a place to stay. She said they were planning to get a hotel room, but I told her Mimi and Bops would love for her to stay at their house. I just needed to overnight her a key since they weren't there. She loved this plan, and I loved that I was able to do something tangible, because it's hard living five hours away and feeling like there's not much you can do to help.

So I got the key to the Houston house from Mimi and Bops, and then drove to the mail store where I paid not a small amount of money to get guaranteed delivery by 10:30 a.m. the next day. And I was none too happy when Jen texted me at noon the following day to let me know the key still hadn't arrived, and they needed to get on the road in the next hour. I immediately drove to the mail store to track down the key and knew I was in trouble when the girl behind the counter typed in the tracking number and said, "I'm going to go get the lady who helped you yesterday." This is normally not a harbinger of glad tidings.

The lady who helped me the day before explained that the package hadn't been scanned again since it left her store the day before, and there was no way to know its current location. That's when all my pent-up feelings from the last forty-eight hours decided to rise to the top and make a fool out of me. I fell apart crying, right there in the mail store among all the people happily mailing their Christmas packages, as I explained the package contained a key for one of my best friends who has cancer. As Gulley said later, I literally went postal at the post office.

It was so bad that the sweet lady in the store wrapped me up in a hug as I cried. She apologized, even though it wasn't her fault, promising me that I could get my money back as soon as the package was located. I called Jen as soon as I got back to the car and started crying again as I told her the key was missing. But then, like we always do, we found the humor in the whole situation. One of my favorite things about Jen has always been that she is quick to find the funny, so I hung up the phone with tears from laughing instead of crying. But then I decided that the delivery company was responsible and should pay for Jen's hotel room in Houston for the night since it was their fault the key was missing and she didn't have a place to stay. I spent the rest of the afternoon emailing back and forth with their customer service department until they agreed to cover the cost of her hotel for the night. Then I made a hotel reservation right in the medical center and texted her the information since she and her husband, Scott, were on their way to Houston at that very moment.

I'm telling you this whole story because as I drove to pick up pizza for dinner later that night, I found myself praying for Jen, thanking God that the delivery company had agreed to cover the cost of her hotel room and asking for the doctors to have wisdom about the best treatments going forward. Then I turned up the radio and heard a Christmas song that includes the words we all know so well: "Do not be afraid, a Savior is born to you this day."

I don't even know what song it was—I had never heard it before—but in that moment, I was hit with the full realization of what Christmas is about. Yes, it's about a baby born to a virgin and laid in a manger. But those words by the angels to those shepherds that night hold the weight of it all: "Do not be afraid, a Savior is born." I've always read those words and just thought of them in terms of the angels reassuring the shepherds there was nothing to fear as they saw a heavenly host in the night sky, which admittedly might cause a person to freak out.

But through the angle of the lens of watching my friend fight this battle with cancer, I saw it as more of a life promise. "Do not be afraid, a Savior is born." Because that's what God gave us when his son Jesus was born that night so long ago: the assurance that we no longer need to be afraid because we have a Savior. We don't need to be afraid of death or the future or the present or all those other fear-mongering rabbit trails our minds go to in the middle of the night when we can't sleep, because we have a God who loves us so much that he sent his son wrapped in the soft skin of a newborn, and what sounded like a baby's cry was actually a holy roar letting darkness know the light will always triumph in the end.

As the weeks went on, Jen saw doctors and had test after test that confirmed she had Stage 4 metastatic breast cancer. We were told she might live anywhere from eighteen to twenty-six months. If there is any silver lining to a cancer diagnosis, it's that it puts what really matters in life into sharp focus. Gulley and I drove from San Antonio to Dallas to be with Jen as she went through the first of many experimental chemotherapy trials. We went to dinner the night before with a whole group of friends who have stuck together in the twenty-plus years since we graduated from Texas A&M, and we laughed and caught up on life until we realized it was almost 10 p.m. and remembered the real reason we were in town was because we had to be at the hospital early the next morning for Jen's treatment.

The days at the hospital were long due to the battery of tests they perform throughout the day. So Jamie met Gulley and me at Starbucks, and then we drove to the hospital to meet Jen. She was getting an initial blood draw, but they eventually moved us into what her nurse referred to as our own private "party room." This seriously oversold what was basically a small patient room, but we were just thankful to have our own little place to set up camp with all our snacks and drinks where we could spend the day together.

And that's what we did. We laughed and told stories and solved problems and had ourselves a complete therapy session before the day was over. We analyzed our marriages, our in-laws, our parents, our clothing choices, and our children. There were moments I almost forgot why we were there until the nurse came in to do a blood draw or Jen's oncologist came in and handed her a "Cancer Sucks" pin to wear. That part? The part where we were all sitting in an oncology ward in a hospital? It still does not compute.

But the thing about being with dear friends is that you can have fun just about anywhere. This was never more evident than when Jen's nurse had to come in and tell us we all needed to be a little quieter because we were laughing and talking too loudly. It just goes to show some things don't change, even when one of you has cancer.

Over the course of the day, different friends stopped by to check on Jen and even brought us lunch. Then Jen's friend Cynthia brought Jen's little boy, Lincoln, up to visit his mama. And he got us all so tickled when he informed us he didn't like Jesus because Jesus has bad hair. Gulley suggested that maybe Jen needed to find a better picture of Jesus to show him in the future, since it's clear the one he's seen might present a Jesus in need of a hairbrush.

It was a short trip, but we packed it full of so many sweet memories and good laughs and the reminder that perhaps nothing makes you realize what's truly important in life more than being with friends you've known and loved for decades. To our great sorrow, none of us had the power to change Jen's circumstances or make the cancer disappear, but we did what we could: loved hard, laughed loud, and hugged like it might be the last time.

At this point, we are now eighteen months into this journey into the unknown. There was a time a few months ago when Jen was in the hospital due to extreme pain and nausea. Gulley and I drove up to visit her and ended up spending that night in the hospital with her just to be close. If I'm honest, I think after we arrived and saw how frail she appeared, we were both afraid it might really be our last time with her. We all tried to act as normal as possible and talked about everything but the fact that Jen was dying of cancer. We discussed school sports, good restaurants, and at one point, what was on sale at Lululemon.

I told Jen about some hot pink workout pants I'd bought on sale for 50 percent off, and she was so intrigued that she had us bring her phone to her so she could see about ordering a pair for herself. As she looked at them online, she said, "Are you sure these are hot pink? Or are they magenta? They look more magenta to me!" I assured her I thought they were more hot pink, so she placed her order, causing Gulley and me to laugh at how a person can be so sick and yet so fundamentally themselves because only Jen would order workout pants from a hospital bed in between waves of pain and nausea.

When it came time for us to drive back to San Antonio, Gulley and I hugged Jen as hard as we could without hurting her, and we all cried our eyes out. I think we all realized this could be our last good-bye, our last moment to say all the things none of us could actually verbalize, except "I love you, I love you, I love you," while the tears became full sobs. But Jen rebounded because she has the strongest will of any person I know, and about ten days later, I received a text from her that said simply, "Got the Lulu pants. THEY COULD NOT BE MORE MAGENTA!" I wanted to tell her I might have known that from the outset but didn't know at the time that she would even live to see them and just knew she'd get some joy from a good bargain.

A few months later, Jen had to travel back to Houston because she had an opportunity to meet with one of the foremost breast cancer doctors in the world. Her cancer has been a medical anomaly in many ways since the very beginning, so it's been difficult to figure out the best treatment options. Gulley and I drove to Houston to meet her there, and we all ended up spending the night at my parents' house, just like we did when we were in college. Jen was actually feeling pretty good, so we were able to go out to dinner and stay up late talking, just like we used to back in the golden days. The next day, after her doctor's appointment was over, we were even able to go shopping at Anthropologie together, and it was hard to even remember she was sick by the way she shopped with us and found cute things for us to try on. We laughed in the dressing room over bad fashion and old memories, and for one brief, shining moment it was like we got the gift of being our twenty-year-old selves again with not a care in the world except finding a good pair of jeans. Then, not even twelve hours later, I became heartbreakingly aware of what a gift that time was. Shortly after they returned home to Dallas, Jen's husband had to rush her to the hospital because she was in such extreme pain. It was another difficult reminder that life can change so quickly and that we need to enjoy each other while we can. I wouldn't trade those hours when God smiled on us and gave us something immeasurable for anything.

Jen is still fighting and has more bad days than good right now. But she's been able to watch her little boy turn five, travel to a few more places, move into a new home, and continually tells everyone how much she trusts in the faithfulness and goodness of God in spite of her circumstances. It has been incredible to see the way her community has supported her family. There have been huge gifts of time, service, and all-expenses paid vacations, but one of the most tangible examples I've seen of absolute love in action is the way our friend Jamie has shown up for Jen during this battle. Jamie and Jen met in junior high and have been best friends ever since. They have that bond you can only have with someone who has known you since the days of braces and bad hair and awkward poetry writing.

While we have all done what we can to help Jen, it's what Jamie has done that stands out to me. There are no grand gestures, just an almost daily faithfulness. Jamie is at every chemo appointment, every late night emergency room visit, and takes care of Jen's little boy, Lincoln, on the days when Jen is fighting too much pain or nausea to take care of him herself. Jamie has sacrificed her time and her own agenda to serve Jen with a million small kindnesses that aren't glamorous, but scream love and devotion in a big way. It's been a reminder that the best thing we can do when someone we love is hurting is show up. Most times there are no right words, no one thing that will make it all better, and nothing we can actually do to change the circumstances.

But we can be the beige wall holding up the neon poster. And make all the difference simply by being there.

After a long, hard battle with cancer, Jen passed away peacefully in her sleep on August 9, 2016. There are no words for how much she impacted everyone who came in contact with her and how much she will be missed. I was able to say one last good-bye before she died, and we both knew it wasn't a forever good-bye as much as an "I'll see you later," but that didn't make it any less painful. I have no doubt she is in heaven with the Savior she loves so dearly. And maybe even offering him some unsolicited advice.

In what is proof to me that God cares about even the smallest details, Jen's beloved ninety-seven-year-old grandmother passed away the Thursday morning after Jen's funeral. The two of them were kindred spirits and ate lunch together every Thursday. I believe God knew Grandma Vonie needed to keep her lunch date with Jen.

Beyond Measure

God has not been trying an experiment on my faith
or love in order to find out their quality. He knew it
already. It was I who didn't. In this trial He makes us
occupy the dock, the witness box, and the bench all
at once. He always knew that my temple was a house
of cards. His only way of making me realize the fact
was to knock it down.

C.S. Lewis

In one form or another, I grew up in the church. Some of my
earliest memories are sitting in a pew while squinting my eyes
to purposely distort all the stained glass images for my own
amusement. I've always been a little bit aware that church, or
"the church," as people like to call it, is a flawed institution at
best, which only makes sense given that it is essentially a human
execution of what God had in mind.

I have laughed at preachers who slam their Bibles on the
pulpit as they promise "hellfire and destruction" in a dramatic
fashion, I have cried over hypocrisy among church members,
I have imitated bad youth group skits where the best looking

boy in the group always plays Jesus and is always so sad at the portrayal of someone at a keg party, I have wrestled with guilt over my lack of desire to serve in children's ministry, and I have wondered endlessly why we sometimes just repeat the same chorus over and over again during worship. But at the heart of it all, I love church. With all its failings and shortcomings and inadequacies, I love the hearts of the people who jump in and do their best to serve and love and follow the heart of God.

Until a year and a half ago, Perry and I attended the same church since Caroline was less than a year old. It was a church we'd had ties to long before that, and it was a great place for us for all those years. We were involved with different ministry groups, learned so much, made new friends. There was a time when I couldn't imagine we'd ever leave to go anywhere else.

But then something began to shift. At first I thought it was just my own issues, but then one night Perry and I talked about it and realized we were feeling the same things. I can't even tell you what the exact feeling was other than just a little bit of restlessness regarding church that we hadn't experienced in a long time. So we began to pray about it and agreed to see what happened next. What happened was that Caroline moved up to the junior high youth group and began to enjoy church more than she ever had during the days of elementary Sunday school. We agreed that was the most important thing and decided it meant we should stay put.

Then, a few weeks later, the youth director sent out an email informing parents that the youth group would no longer meet on Sunday mornings and would meet on Wednesday nights instead. That schedule wasn't going to work for us because the church is about a thirty-minute drive from our house on a Sunday morning and takes even longer when you factor in weekday traffic. Then Caroline admitted that she never really got to know the other kids because none of them were from our neighborhood or attended her school, and what she really wanted was to go to church closer to home.

I remember hearing Priscilla Shirer tell how a mother eagle begins to shake her nest when it's time for her babies to start flying, and I believe that's what was happening to us. Our familiar little nest was being shaken because God was calling us out of our comfort zone. It was one of those times when you're either going to allow God to help you fly, or you're going to fall flat on your face. I have chosen the latter more times than I care to admit.

As we talked about it one night over dinner, what became clear was that all three of us had a desire to attend church in our neighborhood, with the people we go to school with and grocery shop with and see every day. We live in a small community in the middle of San Antonio, and it tends to feel like a small town. We had no doubt God was calling us to be a part of something right here and not thirty minutes away. Our hearts were increasingly drawn close to home. The problem was, we weren't sure there was a church that would be the right fit for us.

Then, one night, as we were discussing it for the twenty-third time, Caroline declared, "Maybe we should start a church!"

What?

No. Just no.

I am not a church plant kind of person. I am not organized. I am not overly spiritual. I have never won a Bible drill contest. I have never even sung in the choir, unless you count my brief stint in Mixed Choir in seventh grade, which sounds much more impressive when I tell you that we sang "Human Nature" by Michael Jackson, complete with extensive hand motion choreography.

So I did the supportive mom thing by essentially patting Caroline on the head and saying, "Aw, that's a sweet idea," while everything inside me was screaming, "PLEASE GOD DON'T MAKE US START A CHURCH! I DON'T WANT TO START A CHURCH!" I knew Perry was thinking exactly the same thing by the way he looked at me across the table.

But it was one of those small things—you know, *those things*—that just burned a hole in my heart and I knew—I KNEW—even though I ignored it, that there was something to it. Out of the mouths of babes and junior high kids and all that.

We spent the next six months after Caroline's declaration visiting different churches in our neighborhood, but none of them seemed right for us. The majority were very traditional, and we just aren't traditional church people. Here's the thing: church preference is such a personal decision. I mean, Gulley and I have never gone to the same church, and she's my best friend and we basically agree on everything, so that's how personal and unique church is to each person. I don't see the fact that we didn't find a good fit as a reflection on any of the churches in our neighborhood as much as the fact that God wanted to create a new, different space. I knew he would eventually wear us down, because Perry and I are ultimately suckers for what God calls us to do, even when we resist at first.

At the same time that this was going on at our house, some acquaintances of ours, August and John, who happen to be immensely talented worship leaders, were feeling called to something new too. August was at another church at the time, and Perry and I just happened to decide to attend that church on

Easter Sunday, specifically because we knew the music would be great. August saw us across the room that morning and came over to say hello. She mentioned that she was feeling restless and believed God was calling her to something new. I stared a hole into the side of Perry's head as August said those words, and I knew at that moment that God was about to do something. I was excited and scared and wonder-filled and nauseous all at the same time. Here's the thing: I have never identified more with Moses when he says, "Oh, my Lord, please send someone else" (Exodus 4:13 ESV).

Perry and I began to watch all the pieces fall into place. Pieces we'd always cited as the reason we could never start a church. Where would we find a good worship leader? Where would we meet? What about the fact that neither of us wanted ministry to be our full-time job? Would anyone even want to come to a new church? What about how I like to sleep in on rainy Sunday mornings? All those things just seemed insurmountable.

I realize now that all of this sounds ridiculous because, well, GOD. It turns out he means it when he says he will do more than we could ask or imagine (Ephesians 3:20). That's why it's more than you can imagine.

Because you can't imagine it.

We met with August and John about a week after Easter and discussed the logistics of what it would take to start a simple Sunday morning worship service. We all agreed that none of us were looking at this as a vocation but rather as creating an organic gathering of people who wanted to come together for worship and teaching with their families each Sunday morning, right in our neighborhood. Kind of like the first churches in Acts, we wanted it to be about the people and not the place. Over the course of the previous year, I'd felt strongly that God was reminding me that the way to change your world is to start in your own community and invest in the lives of the people around you—and that's what we wanted to do. We all gathered in my living room to pray and agreed we would give it thirty days. The thirty-day church experiment.

As I write this, we just celebrated our first year as a church community.

The past year has caused me to question my sanity, my self-ishness, my spirituality, and God. I will confess to at least one or six Sunday mornings when I said out loud to God, "I HATE THIS. I wish you never would have called us to do this" and then ended up in tears an hour later when I looked at the group of people who believe in what we are doing and show up to help us make coffee and set up chairs and greet people as they come through the door. Starting this church or worship service or whatever we call it on any given day has been the greatest and hardest and best and worst thing I have ever done, sometimes all within one five-minute span of time. It has stretched my faith in ways I never imagined and ultimately leaves me feeling so grateful that we have a God who uses us in spite of ourselves.

Several years before any of this happened, I found myself spending a lot of time feeling kind of left out. It seemed as though a lot of people I knew were being used by God to do various things, and I felt like I was a little bit adrift. It was enough to make me feel like I was in fourth grade again and the last one picked for the kickball team. Even though this was different, because it had been years since I'd kicked a big, red rubber ball straight back to the pitcher, making myself what is known as an easy out. Which only actually happened twice, by the way. But fourth graders are an unforgiving bunch with a long memory where kickball is concerned.

The thing about feeling left out is it turns into some sort of quicksand of self-doubt. What's wrong with me? Am I not a likable person? Is it because I'm socially awkward? Am I not good enough? Is it because I admit to watching every season of *The Bachelor*? Do people think I'm shallow?

Then I would catch a glimpse of myself in the mirror and lose my train of thought because I'd notice a new gray hair, which inevitably led to a full evaluation of the state of my eyebrows.

No way anyone thinks I'm shallow.

So basically, I was struggling with all these feelings of being inadequate and questioning why things happen the way they do and wondering why I wasn't good enough for this or that.

One night I climbed into bed, and my mind was racing with all these things I'd perceived as slights, and I began to get all worked up. All my doubts and fears came flying to the surface until I felt like I wanted to cry.

At that moment, I felt God speak to my heart, saying, "You need to quit asking 'Why?' and start asking me 'Where?'" I knew immediately it was God because I wouldn't have come up with anything that profound. And I certainly wouldn't have come up with anything that succinct.

I realized I'd fallen into a cycle of asking, "Why not me?" or "Why me?" or "Why is this so hard?" and now it was time for me to ask, "Where would you have me go? Where would you have me serve? Where are you leading me?"

Don't get me wrong. I think there is a time to ask why. I have friends who are facing hard circumstances, the kinds of things that can only lead them to question why. I think God understands our need to ask why at times, even if he doesn't always give us the answer. He isn't afraid of our questions.

But my "Why?" had become a question that was causing me to spiral into a vat of self-pity, which is even more gross than a vat of tartar sauce. It's hard to admit, because even now I'd like to think I'm better than that.

Asking "Where?" changes things. It takes the focus off me and what I perceive as my failures and shortcomings and all the ways I don't measure up and puts the focus where it belongs. On God. The One who has plans and purposes for us, in spite of all our failures and fears.

Then you realize the why doesn't really matter as much as the where. The where is the question that asks, "What am I supposed to be doing?" instead of the why that always seems to ask, "What am I doing wrong?"

The world tells us we have to do it all, be it all, and achieve it all. We need to do big, important things to leave a legacy. All while looking fabulous and being a size four and raising kids who are fluent in at least two languages and in gifted classes. Our houses have to be straight out of Pinterest, our dinners need to be clean and healthy, and our Instagram accounts should to be full of beautifully filtered photos that catch every single moment of our kids' lives or they'll end up in therapy wondering why they don't have an Instagram book like all the other kids.

We are a generation of women who have never worked harder to have it all, yet go to bed most nights worrying that we aren't enough. We are constantly asking "Why?" We are constantly measuring. It doesn't matter if you're single, if you're married, if you're rich, poor, old, young, in college, or out of college. Every human heart struggles with this. We are always looking around to see how we measure up to everyone around us and usually focusing on all the ways we fall short.

I believe our struggle with wondering if we are enough goes back primarily to how much we trust God. We aren't struggling because of the specifics of our circumstances as much as we are struggling because we fail to trust God to give us what we need, to show us where we are supposed to go and what we are supposed to do. That's why discontentment surfaces in our lives in all the ways it does.

Deep down, we struggle to believe God is going to lead us to what is best for us. It's our internal voice that whispers we will never be enough, so we work and worry and feel like we must do something big, something huge to prove our worth and to make sure our life matters. We have to host a conference, start a movement, adopt fifteen kids, or fight human trafficking to really matter. Which are all great things, but thinking this way can cause us to lose sight of the small things that can also change a life: bringing dinner to a sick neighbor, smiling at a waitress who's having a bad day, reading to your kids before bed, and simply praying for someone going through a rough time.

If you're like me, you can spend a lot of time looking around at what everyone else has or is doing or all the ways they appear better. We measure. We measure our insides by other people's outsides—and that's never a fair assessment. We don't know what they're going through, how they have been hurt, or the struggles they face. We see their social-media best selves and assume everybody is winning at life. We are constantly seeing the "Everything's great!" version of other people's lives while living the reality of our own lives, which may often feel a little mundane and purposeless.

A few weeks ago, as I was reading my Bible, I ran across some verses that leapt out at me. I can't even explain how I found myself in Zechariah, because sometimes I can't remember if it's a real book of the Bible or one I made up in my head because Zechariah *sounds* like a name that would be a book of the Bible. I read:

> And I lifted my eyes and saw, and behold, a man with a measuring line in his hand! Then I said, "Where are you going?" And he said to me, "To measure Jerusalem, to see what is its width and what is its length." And behold, the angel who talked with me came forward, and another angel came forward to meet him and said to him, "Run, say to that young man, 'Jerusalem shall be inhabited as villages without walls, because of the multitude of people and livestock in it. And I will be to her a wall of fire all around, declares the LORD, and I will be the glory in her midst.'" (Zechariah 2:1–5 ESV)

It hit me that this is what we spend so much time doing. We are constantly measuring our city—is it big enough? Does it need more? How does it compare to other cities? Does my city have the kitchen that looks most likely to get pinned on Pinterest? Do people like my city?

I wonder what might happen if we could quit building walls around ourselves and let others see who we really are. To see where we are broken and where we are hurting and where we feel like we aren't enough. Sometimes when we speak those things out loud, they lose their power, but when we keep them hidden, they grow stronger because we are almost always our own worst critics.

What if we lived as though we truly believed God has given us a life without walls, that he has plans for us that go beyond anything we can measure or imagine and promises to be the glory in our midst?

I believe God wants to make our city—our lives—so big that walls can't contain it. His idea of big is so different from ours. A God who promises us that not even a sparrow falls to the ground without him knowing is a God who values even the smallest things. He wants us to have peace and contentment that won't require us to put up walls of protection and spend our lives afraid of being vulnerable and real as we stop compulsively trying to measure the width and depth of our lives. He will be our protection. He will be the wall of fire all around. He will be the glory in our midst and whisper to us that our lives, no matter how small they may seem to us, are enough because he is enough.

I used to be a member of the Church of Big Moments. I lived for the major life events, the magnanimous gestures, and the idea that the best marriage proposals surely happen on the fifty-yard line at halftime during a football game. Because what says happily ever after more than fifteen seconds of fame on a Jumbotron? Unless, of course, it's Tom Cruise busting into a room full of women and declaring, "You complete me."

In that funny way life has of teaching you as you go, I learned over the years that it's usually not the big moments that make up a life as much as it is the small ones. It's not going to college and setting up a dorm room that makes you an adult but the discipline of showing up for class, studying for tests, and learning that perhaps Jell-O shots are a bad idea. It's not the wedding ceremony that makes you a married couple, but the daily commitment to stay in love even when someone is seemingly incapable of throwing away the wrappers from the York Peppermint Patties he eats every night and asks every year if Valentine's Day is the second Tuesday in February. It's not giving birth or signing adoption papers that makes you a mom, but braiding hair and kissing scraped knees and walking the floor at night with a feverish baby in your arms as you whisper a silent prayer, or listening to someone sound out the word "cat" until you want to gnaw your arm off to make it stop. I've learned that the best way to live is to look for God in the church of small things. The church of small things is where God does his best work. The church of small things is where the majority of us live every single day.

Vincent van Gogh said, "Man, I really wish I hadn't cut my ear off" (probably) but he also said, "Great things are done by a series of small things brought together." That's it. Or in the equally profound lyrics of the classic TV show *One Day at a Time*, "This is it, this is life, the one you get, so go and have a ball."

Acknowledgments

Writing a book is a funny thing because it can be such a lonely process to have to live inside your own head for months on end, but at the same time you have a whole support system who is cheering you on and praying for you every step of the way. They remind you to breathe, to keep engaging in life, and to shower. They assure you the book you're working on won't be the worst thing ever written and always seem to say the right thing just when you feel like you're on the edge. At some point in the middle of writing each book I've written, I wonder why I do this to myself. Why do I subject myself to this crazy-making endeavor? The following people are the reason why.

Perry: You are the calm in my storm. When I think everything might be terrible, you remind me that life always has a way of working out and that I need to fight for what I believe in. You never fail to support everything I do, even when it means a lot of takeout dinners and being down to our last roll of toilet paper. You are home to me, and I love you more now than I did twenty years ago.

Caroline: You are all my dreams come true. I didn't even know what I hoped my daughter would be, but you have surpassed anything I could have imagined. I am so proud of you and can't wait to see what God continues to do in your life. You have a heart for him that inspires me every day.

Mimi and Bops: There aren't even words for the love and support you have given me over the years. You have both cheered me on and supported this crazy dream every step of the way. I wouldn't be who I am without the two of you. I love you both so much.

Lisa Jackson: I trusted you with my writing career from the very beginning, first as a publisher and now as an agent, and you have never let me down. You encourage me, challenge me, and make me laugh every step of the way. Thank you for reminding me to always trust my instincts. You are more than an agent; you are a dear friend, and I am so grateful for you.

The Zondervan Team: I am not a girl who enjoys change, and I was a little afraid of what it would be like to work with a new publishing group. But from the moment I arrived in Grand Rapids and saw that Jesus was wearing a Texas A&M shirt, I knew you were my people. I cannot thank you enough for all the ways you have embraced this project and worked hard to make it more than I could have hoped for. I love that every time I said, "Maybe we could . . .", you were always up for the challenge and figured out a way to make it happen.

Acknowledgments

Amy: I'm so thankful that I was given both a sister and a friend in one package. Thanks for loving me, encouraging me, and making me laugh.

Gulley: Thanks for all the money you have saved me on therapy bills. You always know whether a crisis of faith or identity or parenting calls for chocolate chip cookies or wine or, most likely, both. Nobody's cuter than you.

Jamie: Watching the way you loved and cared for Jen made me want to be a better version of myself. I'm forever thankful you're in my top five. (Or four. Sorry, Trevor.)

Sophie: No one can help me edit, outline, or think about a better way to write something than you. It's so handy to have a former English teacher as one of your dearest friends, and I am so grateful for all the ways you help and encourage me and make me feel less crazy.

Beth Moore: I don't know that I ever would have written one word if not for your influence in my life. The fact that God used your Bible studies to change me forever and then actually put you in my life as a real-life mentor is one of his most outrageous blessings to me.

Ree Drummond: Thank you for your encouragement and advice and for taking the time to write the foreword for this book. You are always so faithful to support me, and I appreciate it so much.

My blog readers: The fact that you have faithfully shown up in my little corner of the world wide web for over eleven years now is just crazy. Thank you for reading my words, loving my family, and reminding me that sometimes what we all need is a good laugh. I am eternally grateful for each and every one of you.

And, most of all, God: You gave me a gift for writing words, and I will use it forever to bring glory to your name. You are the great love of my life. My prayer is that I will use every bit of every small thing you've put in my path to point back to your great love and faithfulness.

100 Devotions to Find a Big God in the Little Moments

It is a rite of passage for every woman: the day you wake up and say, *"Wait, THIS is the life I signed up for?!?"* We've all been there—Melanie Shankle is just brave enough to say it out loud. *Everyday Holy* is your invitation to reexamine your life and find the beautiful little pieces that create a picture of a beautiful big God.

Available March 2018